nuing

A

Century

1910-2010

OF HOSPITALITY

American Hotel & Lodging Association

CELEBRATING 100 YEARS OF HOSPITALITY
CONTINUING THE LEGACY

Library of Congress Cataloging-in-Publication Data
Library of Congress Control Number: 2009928450
ISBN 978-0-86612-350-1 (hardcover)

Edited by McNeill Group Inc., Yardley, PA
Editor: Len Vermillion
Managing Editor: Marla Cimini

Published by the American Hotel and Lodging Association

Designed by Shane P. Hickey, McNeill Group Inc., Yardley, PA
The text of this book is set both in Caslon 224 and The Sans. The display is in Archer.
Back cover image: The Palmer House, Chicago, Illinois

Printed by Cadmus Communications, a Cenveo Company

First Edition

a Century
OF HOSPITALITY
1910-2010

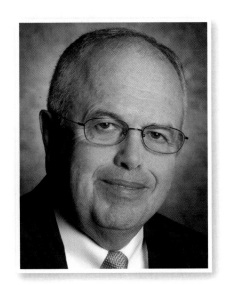

100 Years of Service

The American Hotel & Lodging Association (AH&LA) celebrates a monumental milestone in 2010, our Centennial Anniversary. It gives us an opportunity to reflect on the innovative and illustrious history of our industry, its growth and accomplishments throughout our nation, and focus on its future. Looking back to 1910, there were less than 10,000 hotels nationwide, the average room rate was $2 per night, and allowing income taxes was the biggest issue on Capitol Hill. Hoteliers were worried about fraud, crooks, and deadbeats wreaking havoc on their businesses. It was a time of change and uncertainty, and hoteliers knew they needed to work together to overcome their common challenges. Thus, the American Hotel Protective Association was founded. It would change its name three times before settling on the American Hotel & Lodging Association (AH&LA) in 2002. Although times have changed tremendously, the core objective of providing the public with safe, comfortable accommodations, and quality service has remained at the heart of the lodging industry, and the driving force behind all of AH&LA's actions. Hotels are more than a home away from home for travelers, they are the focal point of the community, they provide refuge and relief to those in need when they truly need it the most. During natural disasters and national catastrophes, hotels always rise to the occasion as servants to their community. Evaluating our first 100 years as an association, it's appropriate not only to celebrate the leaders and visionaries, innovations, and events that have made our industry what it is today, but to also look forward to the next 100 years as a continuation of our legacy, one which builds a better tomorrow for all those that the hotel industry touches.

— Joseph A. McInerney, CHA
President/CEO, American Hotel & Lodging Association

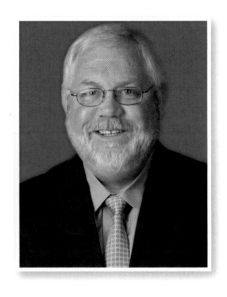

Growing Together

During its first 100 years, AH&LA developed into an industry juggernaut that STR is proud to partner with on many levels. AH&LA serves as the voice for the U.S. hotel industry, and its presence has been felt across a wide spectrum of issues over the years. Its influence on the educational, operational, and governmental aspects of the hotel industry cannot be underestimated. STR also is celebrating a milestone in 2010. It's been 25 years since we first formed in Lancaster, Pennsylvania, and much like AH&LA, we recognize the importance of adapting to new ideas and technologies. About 24 years ago, we approached Ken Hine, the CEO of the association at that time, about endorsing our monthly survey. He agreed, and we have been working closely with AH&LA ever since. Also, STR — in conjunction with Deloitte and The Bench — has established STR Global to bring the transparency and knowledge of data to the hotel industry. More information can be found at www.strglobal.com. In addition, STR has launched two other initiatives. Its Hotel Data Conference is a unique gathering that focuses on delving deep into the data that drives the hotel industry. HotelNewsNow.com, a digital news and information platform, was launched as a means to disseminate important information to the global hotel industry. It's with great pride that we at STR congratulate AH&LA on its 100 years of groundbreaking leadership that has guided our industry through triumph and tragedy.

— Randall A. Smith
Co-founder and CEO, STR

American Express Company
CREDIT CARD
EXPIRES APRIL 30, 1959

Account Number → 201 002 730 0

JOHN J SMITH
123 MAIN STREET
CENTERVILLE USA

AUTHORIZED SIGNATURE - NOT TRANSFERABLE
SEE REVERSE SIDE

IBM

© A.E.CO.

Supporting Travel and Tourism

American Express is committed to supporting travel industry associations and has been a leading corporate sponsor of the American Hotel and Lodging Association (AH&LA) for more than 50 years. We at American Express would like to congratulate AH&LA on its centennial anniversary, a remarkable achievement. We are proud to partner with AH&LA on a number of lodging industry programs, including educational opportunities for industry members and the ongoing support of the lodging industry. For more than a century, American Express has partnered with suppliers, travel agents, and associations to help nurture a strong travel and tourism industry. We are proud to help our partners expand their business opportunities by preserving, protecting, and promoting travel and tourism worldwide. American Express Company is a diversified worldwide travel, financial, and network services company founded in 1850. It is a world leader in charge and credit cards, Travelers Cheques, travel, financial planning, business services, insurance, and international banking. For more information on American Express and its work in promoting travel and tourism, please visit www.americanexpress.com.

— Shane Berry
Senior Vice President &
General Manager
National Client Group
American Express

INTRODUCTION

In **1910**,
60 hotel
operators formed
the **American
Hotel Protective
Association.**

For modern-day travelers, it's often easy to take hotels for granted. No matter which city, town, or area one travels to, they are usually able to find lodging. But what travelers might not realize is that while hotels are commonplace today, they weren't in 1910. Today, there are more than 50,000 hotels in the United States, but 100 years ago, there was less then one-fifth as many across the country. And, at the time, nearly all were independently run operations whose existence depended on "walk-in" guests and cash payments. With no telephones, computers, or pre-payment by credit card options available, this was often a risky endeavor, as hoteliers at the beginning of the last century were plagued by deadbeat guests who skipped out on hotel bills and criminals who stole from both guestrooms and public spaces. What's more, hotel owners and operators dealt with many other issues, both social and economic, over the course of the early century that significantly threatened their businesses. Shortly after the turn of the 20th century, the hospitality industry, like many others, was fraught with challenges. Making matters worse, most hoteliers of the time had nowhere to turn for aid in combating these challenges, and their independent voices where often not loud enough for help to hear.

Built in the 1920s, the Hay-Adams hotel near the White House has been part of a wide range of events throughout American history.

That all began to change in 1910, however. On January 31 of that year, a small group of midwestern hoteliers gathered at the Palmer House in Chicago, Illinois, for a think tank session to address their primary concerns — how to protect themselves against the deadbeat guests who often left them short-changed when it came time to pay for their stays and the thieves who found their hotels prime targets.

At that meeting, they decided to ban together to figure out ways to protect themselves. At the end of the meeting, they had officially formed the American Hotel Protective Association. A few months later, they expanded to the East, and a national association was born. Soon after, its initial charter of providing protection for hoteliers would expand to address many other issues ranging from government legislation to hotel standards to the sharing of knowledge and business practices.

That small association, which consisted of approximately 60 members in 1910, was the beginning of what is today known as — after three name changes over the course of time — the American Hotel & Lodging Association (AH&LA). The modern-day AH&LA represents more than 11,000 hoteliers in the United States.

After operating under its original moniker and then as the American Hotel & Motel Association (AH&MA) through the latter half of the century, AH&LA is the only national association representing all sectors and stakeholders in the lodging industry, including individual hotel property members, hotel companies, student and faculty members, and industry suppliers. Headquartered in Washington, D.C., AH&LA provides members with national advocacy on Capitol Hill, public relations and image management, education, research and information, and other value-added services to provide bottom-line savings and to ensure a positive business climate for the entire lodging industry.

Modern-day hotels, of course, are a far cry from the indepenently operated properties that dominated the industry in 1910. With the building of the nation's highway system in the middle part of the 20th century through the rise of affordable airplane travel later in more modern times, travel has become an integral part of American life — for business and leisure activities. It has also become a vital part of the American economy. And, with the improvements in travel convenience, came changes to hotels. Nowadays, there are many different types of hotels from which American consumers can choose — everything from roadside motels to urban "boutique" hotels to luxury resorts.

Throughout its existence, the association has been an strong advocate for the lodging industry, and it has seen the industry through both economic and societal changes. Most important, it has taken a central role in helping the lodging industry grow over the course of the last 100 years.

Chairmen of AH&LA
1940-2010

1925-1940
Thomas Dismukes Green

1940s

Franklin Moore
1941

Bruce E. Anderson
1942

Harold Van Orman
1943

Glenwood J. Sherrard
1944

J.E. Frawley
1945

Leonard Hicks, Sr.
1947

Howard F. Dugan
1948

Joseph H. Adams
1949

1950s

T. Harry Gowman
1950

Daniel J. O'Brien
1951

J.B. Herndon Jr.
1952

Arthur J. Packard
1953

Albert Pick Jr.
1954

Tom L. Powell
1955

Les Carter
1956

Earl A. Johnson
1957

Seymour Weiss
1957

Maillard Bennett
1958

Edwin A. Boss
1959

1960s

Vernon Herndon
1960

C.J. Mack
1961

Randall L. Davis
1962

John D. Green
1963

Roy Watson
1964

Willard E. Abel
1965

James T. McFate
1966

William J. Burns
1967

Ed C. Leach
1968

Creighton D. Holden
1969

1970s

Herbert C. Blunck
1970

Robert A. Riedel
1971

George D. Johnson
1972

J. Frank Birdsall Jr.
1973

Paul R. Handlery
1974

Harry Mullikon
1975

Paul D. Galeese
1976

Richard E. Holtzman
1977

Neil R. Messick Jr.
1978

Porter P. Parris
1979

1980s

Philip Pistilli
1980

John A. Brooke
1981

Douglass L. Fontaine
1982

J. Q. Jack Masteller
1983

Tom F. Herring Sr.
1984

Howard P. James
1985

William H. Edwards
1986

Donald E. Jankura
1987

Thomas W. Staed
1988

Elaine G. Etess
1989

1990s

Roger A. Saunders
1990

Richard C. Nelson
1991

David B. Kenney
1992

M.O. "Bus" Ryan
1993

Michael Peceri
1994

Gene Rupnik
1995

Curtis G. Williams
1996

Jonathan Tisch
1997

Valerie C. Ferguson
1998

Hasmukh P. Rama
1999

2000s

Robert E. Slater
2000

John J. Russell, Jr.
2001

Kirby Payne
2002

Michael K. Handlery
2003

Dieter Huckestein
2004

Pedro Mandoki
2005

Joseph R. Kane, Jr.
2006

Robert L. Steele, III
2007

Thomas J. Corcoran Jr.
2008

Joe Martin
2009

David Kong
2010

In 1910, a group of hoteliers assembled at the Palmer House in Chicago where they founded the American Hotel Protective Association.

1910-1919

The Sky's the Limit

by Philip Hayward

To be a hotelier in the decade beginning in 1910 meant to be front and center of an immense whirlpool of social and economic trends. Seen in continuum, it was an era of remarkable innovation and social upheaval that would involve hotels at nearly every level. This was the year of Comet Halley, the death of Mark Twain, and the birth of Mother Theresa. Railroads were crisscrossing the country at the same time as air travel was becoming a reality. Massive waves of Europeans were reshaping U.S. labor. Labor unions became a force to be reckoned with. Women's rights gained traction and would soon blossom into the 19th Amendment at the end of the decade. Traveling salesman, or "drummers" as they were then called, were coalescing into a constituency in their own right. Safer, faster transatlantic travel meant Americans could readily vacation overseas, prompting the rise of travel advocacy programs exhorting travelers to "See America First."

Thanks to building construction innovations, skyscrapers housed hotels and their elevators whisked guests to unheard-of heights. In their rooms, guests had electric lighting and plumbing. By 1910, the great shift from European meal plans to the a la carte American plans were revolutionizing hotel dining. New York City's St. Regis Hotel provided cooling units in guestrooms. The Hotel Statler chain had begun just two years earlier and offered, in addition to private rooms and baths, full-length mirrors, telephones, and built-in radios — all of which would serve as the model for hotel design for the next 40 years.

But with all this progress came issues and problems that only organiza-tions of hotel executives could handle. Perennial among issues was the matter of deadbeat guests who simply failed to pay for their stays. As the railway network expanded, it made it easier for the miscreant traveler to skip town and repeat the process all over again in distant cities. Or they could simply try another hotel in the same town, since few organized communications mechanisms existed. And, other issues abounded that required associated effort by hoteliers.

Establishing lodging trade associations interestingly began with considerable pressure and organizing effort from what today would seem like an unlikely source — the newly formed hotel trade press. Editors served side by side with hoteliers in the early history of the formation of the associations. Often, they were out in front of a variety of issues and trends, pushing industry leaders for change.

The *National Hotel Register* in Chicago, under the ownership of F. Willis Rice and James W. Scott, stood out among an increasingly crowded field of hotel publications, beginning in 1871. (Other publications included *Hotel World*, *Western Hotel Reporter*, and the *Hotel Gazette*. At one point, St. Louis, Missouri, could lay claim to having three daily

The first Radisson Hotel opened in Minneapolis, Minnesota, in 1909.

- The **American Hotel Protective Association** is founded in Chicago.

- The **U.S. Grant Hotel** opens in San Diego on the site of the original Horton House hotel.

- Margaret J. Anderson and her son, Stanley S. Anderson, open **The Beverly Hills Hotel.**

- The **Copley Plaza** is built on the original site of the Museum of Fine Arts in Boston.

- **The Greenbrier Hotel** opens at a West Virginia resort where generations of travelers "take the sulfur water" for their health. The previous resort consisted only of rows of cottages.

1910   **1911**   **1912**   **1913**   **1914**

hotel newspapers, prompting a publisher in Chicago to wonder "where it all would end." But it was Rice and Scott who yielded the most influence in the industry and who would ultimately help create what would become the organization known as the American Hotel & Lodging Association. In 1877 or 1878 (nobody's sure of which year), the two men formed the earliest hotel association in the country, the Chicago Hotel Association. Although social in nature and by law (Illinois law forbade such associations from engaging in business), the CHA took on the role of "mutual protection." But the fledgling association folded after two years. Rice and Scott, however, next pursued creation of the Hotel Association of New York City. Within a year, under Scott's influence, the Hotel Men's Mutual Benefit Association launched in 1879, becoming the first national hotel association.

On January 31, 1910, a group of Midwestern hoteliers met in the Palmer House in Chicago to found a new national association, with "protection" written in as its core mission, particularly from deadbeat guests. Most of the people from this group had begun their hotel careers working in small hotels where they were raised, or were sons of hoteliers,

accidental hoteliers, and the trade press (which comprised 20 percent of the participants of the founding meeting.) Few had college educations. Their chief organizer was the German immigrant, Max Teich, a hotelier trained in the classical manner in his home country. He eventually became owner of the Kaiserhof Hotel in Chicago.

Their first meeting convened in August 1910 and included a few Easterners, most notaby E.M. Statler, whose stature was rapidly increasing with each new hotel he built. While the American Hotel Men's Protective Association (AHMPA) constitution specified protection against deadbeats, it left room for compromise with those who thought a national trade organization should champion other causes. There was no shortage of people wanting the organization to go in a different direction.

Traveling salesmen had formed their own organization pushing for

Built in 1909, in Oregon, The Governor Hotel's Renaissance Ballroom was the site of many functions.

improvements on a variety of concerns, from safety and cleanliness to American-style dining plans, which they abhorred. The Hotel & Restaurant Employees Union had formed 20 years earlier as an affiliate of Samuel Gompers' American Federation of Labor. The Interstate Commerce Act passed Congress in 1888 and immediately began generating government's interest in railroad-owned hotels. Economic cycles, such as the devastating Panic of 1893, only increased hoteliers' worries of fraud.

While state hotel associations enjoyed considerable success by the turn of the century, national organizing still suffered from pervasive top-down thinking. It had been hard to encourage the participation of state association executives in matters of interstate commerce. Even as the Prohibition movement spread among the states like wildfire and as rumblings about increased government regulation of matters as small as whether hoteliers should be serving food at all, state associations continued to go their own ways. Travel promotion and the creation of a uniform law based on the exceedingly difficult definition of what precisely constituted a hotel were much needed. That was the lot facing the first

In 1912, the Copley Plaza was built on the site of Boston's Museum of Fine Arts.

elected president of the AHMPA, Sam Dutton, proprietor of the Albany Hotel Company in Denver, Colorado.

While the new association enjoyed immediate success in apprehending criminals through the efforts of the security firm it contracted, the Thiel Agency, these other issues continued to push at AHMPA. To the 21st century mind, some issues border on the ludicrous — New York's state legislature was even seriously considering a measure stipulating, "that no automobile could cross the border into New York State without being registered in the state." The threat of that bill led to widespread hotel cancelations. The hotel industry had to consider the merits of proposed federal interstate commerce protection — still a remote long shot to pass in Congress, considering the avid states-right leanings of early AHMPA members.

The 1910s were also a decade of widespread labor organizing, which would have a significant impact on hotel operators. In that period came the International Stewards Association (ISA), the International Geneva Association, the Greeters of America, the United Commercial Travelers, the International Housekeepers Association, the Negro Workers Benevolent Association, the Japanese Hotel Keepers Association, the Pacific Coast Waiters Association, and Hotel Women (formed by the wives of Los Angeles hotelmen.) By 1910 three women were serving on the board of the Denver Hotel Association. In fact, the role of women in lodging was quickly growing and by the end of the decade was considered significant.

E.M. Statler:
Creator of the Modern Hotel

By Philip Hayward

Before E.M. Statler, there really were hotels. But that is like saying there were cars before Henry Ford. Lodging before the turn of the century had neither the heart, soul, or vision that the Pennsylvania native brought to the hotel industry. Hotels prior to Statler's era made money, but they lacked the dreamer's touch for innovation. By the time he died in 1928, at the age of 65, his hotels comprised a chain. They provided private bathrooms with running water, tubs, and showers; radios in every room; parking garages; libraries (one property held 3,000 volumes); and improved working conditions (six-day work weeks, paid holidays, free health coverage, and profit-sharing.) They also had a strict, structured code of hospitality service. It was one thing to go from rags to riches, but it was another matter altogether to leave such a positive, indelible legacy.

E.M. (he preferred the simplicity of initials to Ellsworth Milton) Statler was born in 1863 near Gettysburg, Pennsylvania. He was the son of Mary Ann McKinney and William Jackson Statler, a pastor. A year later, the eight members of the Statler family moved to Bridgeport, Ohio. In nearby Kirkwood, Ohio, nine-year-old E.M. entered the workforce, toiling in the sweltering depths of the La Belle Glass Works. His 50 cent per day wages were meant to support his family. But at age 12 and earning 90 cents a day, Statler left La Belle to take a pay cut across the Ohio River at the McClure House, a hotel in Wheeling, West Virginia, that paid him $6 a month as a bellboy. Poor and uneducated, Statler was nevertheless a shrewd observer and climber. The McClure's bartender taught him proper English and from guests he learned manners and mannerisms. He studied the hotel's shortcomings: Rooms in first-class offered only a washstand, pitcher and basin, a dresser, and a bed. It was also a window on the world of opportunity, and Statler learned how to operate concessions for hotels, which allowed him to save money for larger projects.

His first major venture, a restaurant on the ground floor of the Ellicott Square Building in Buffalo, New York, almost failed before catching on. He soon was able to build temporary hotels for international expositions and finally his first permanent hotel in Buffalo in 1907 — the Statler. Others followed in quick succession: Cleveland (1,000 rooms) in 1912, Detroit (1,000 rooms) in 1915, St. Louis (650 rooms) in 1917, and New York City (the Pennsylvania, with 2,200 rooms) in 1919. When the decade closed, the Statler chain of five hotels had 5,300 rooms, 4,700 employees, 6,700 guests a day, and an annual gross revenue of $2.5 million. ●

Other Notables

● **Sam Dutton**
A Colorado hotelier, he was the first president of the American Hotel Protective Association. As president of the association, he championed a "See America First" campaign.

● **E.M. Tierney**
Even before AHA was formed, local hoteliers began to organize as early as the late 1800s. Tierney became a force in the industry from his role as president of the State Hotel Keepers' Association of New York.

Training and education, always an afterthought before 1910, quickly gained importance as an issue. As Americans increasingly traveled the globe, they considered American hotels superior in physical plant but

Oscar Tschirky, the renowned maitre d' of the Waldorf=Astoria (standing, sixth from left) was known for hosting industry gatherings, such as this one at his New Paltz, N.Y., farm in 1916.

Oscar's restaurant at the Waldorf=Astoria is named for Tschirky, creator of Veal Oscar and the Waldorf Salad.

far inferior to the service offered in Europe. With no university training programs, technical institutes nor secondary school offerings in the United States to prepare a new generation of hotel leaders, low service levels were likely to continue.

Beginning in 1910, however, ISA, under the auspices of its president, Fred Klooz, began deliberations for creation of a two-year training program based on a similar program already in place in Paris, France. Klooz sought $200,000 from hoteliers and associations around the country. Realizing his intended school could not train persons for every position, Klooz instead figured his program would turn out managers with "char-

acter, efficiency, and self-discipline instilled in them."

Unfortunately, Klooz and ISA never got very far. But momentum picked up on the college level, where hoteliers protested public monies being spent on agriculture, education, and home economics in state universities. Home economics, interestingly, would eventually illuminate the route of the creation of the first university hotel programs. In the meantime, learning on the job would continue to be the primary method of training hotel employees.

But the industry would get religion between 1911 and 1916 as labor strife began to close in. And when war broke out in Europe in 1914, U.S. hotel operators found their sources of European-trained department heads and lower-level executives dried up. And many of the Europeans already working in U.S. hotels returned to their native lands to fight.

Some groundwork for a hotel curriculum was being laid in 1911 when Columbia University and New York University began offering home economics courses to people interested in hotel work, since much of the subject matter overlapped with lodging

A New View of Travel

by Marla Cimini

The early 1900s proved to be an exciting time of transition in hospitality, as a number of major innovations impacted the industry in a variety of areas. The industrial revolution was winding down, but its widespread influence was still in high gear, and drastically altered the way people traveled. Most important, it forever changed how travelers looked at the world.

Innovative technologies certainly played a key role in the progress of engineering and construction improvements throughout the United States, such as the introduction of machine-based manufacturing and steam power, but several other enhancements directly affected hotels.

Guests seeking climate control were thrilled in 1904, when the St. Regis in New York City became the first hotel to offer individually controlled heating and air-conditioning units in each room. At the time, air-conditioning was considered a luxury, as it had been invented a mere two years earlier — in 1902.

Another advancement was the enhancement of hotel bathrooms. Until this time, hotels featured shared hallway facilities for a number of guestrooms. The first hotel to feature private bathrooms in each room was the Statler Hotel, which opened in 1908 in Buffalo, New York, and became the gold standard for hotel innovations for years to come. At this establishment, guests also enjoyed the added benefit of full-length mirrors, private phones in each room, and built-in radios. This hotel's modern engineering was also ahead of its time, as the Statler Plumbing Shaft is still used in construction today.

Transportation also made an impact on the travel world during this time. Mass production of the automobile began in this era, which along with the Federal Road Act introduced in 1916, brought a sudden, new convenience to road travel. This later created a major boom in the hotel industry, and led to the development of small motor hotels (motels) along the U.S. highways. Not surprisingly, the Wright Brothers' first airplane flight in 1903 became another catalyst for eventually creating and changing the style of the way travelers trek the globe. ●

Early 1900s

● **Luggage labels** (shown) became a popular status symbol for travelers and were eagerly used as an advertising tool for hotels around the world.

1900

● Boston's **Lenox Hotel** opened with the first **shower bath** and **roof garden**. This hotel also introduced travelers to American/European lodging plans for **$2**.

● **Kodak introduced** the $1 "Brownie" camera, making photography available **to travelers everywhere**.

1908

● The first **Gideon's Bible** was placed in the Superior Hotel in Iron Mountain, Montana.

● Hotel Statler in Buffalo, New York, was the first to provide **slots in guestroom doors** that conveniently allowed daily newspapers to easily slip through. That same year, the hotel also introduced **circulating ice water** and **single-handed lavoratory faucets** in guestrooms.

● Ford introduced **the Model T** car and paved the way for auto travel across the United States. Automobile travel spurred the **growth of the motel industry**.

operations. So popular among males were the home economics courses at Cornell University that the department's administrators banned males from the female-taught classes.

It's difficult in the first decade of the 21st century to appreciate the level of passion among hoteliers over the simple act of preparing and serving a meal a century ago. Hoteliers in 1910 nevertheless were practitioners of a distinctly American approach to food and beverage that was more suited to small town life than large cities. Today, it would be called the "American Plan," where meals are served family style and whose cost is included in the room charge. That was fine by all — until the second half of the 19th century when socio-economic forces and trends began to challenge this simple concept.

The Grand Staircase of the Palmer House in Chicago, Illinois.

Thanks to safer and faster transatlantic travel, Americans set off to Europe in greater numbers and were treated to meals prepared a la carte and served at individual tables. Called the "European Plan," it was more than enough to give U.S. hotel operators financial and logistical indigestion. At the turn of the century, hotel owners preferred to keep the number of meal servers to a minimum, which was possible when all the guests sat down at the same table at the same time to consume whatever was put in front of them. Many considered such service a hallmark of democratic American society. Increasing numbers of Americans returning from Europe saw it differently and demanded their own tables and the freedom to custom order their meals. The European plan required smaller tables and servers who could read and calculate, and provide warm and hospitable service that would partially be compensated by the foreign custom of tipping. It created an entirely new dimension of cost accounting, a primitive discipline at that point in the U.S. hotel industry.

Even though many hoteliers adopted European-style dining, they quickly found out that it wasn't always enough to keep their guests in-house to take their meals. Quickly fading were the social taboos among "the right kind of people" about dining in stand-alone restaurants. But hoteliers identified this emerging trend and quickly acted. Chief among them were E.M. Statler in Buffalo and Charles Rector in Chicago, both of whom profitably created their own stand-alone lunch rooms. They may have been prompted by the success and subsequent expansion of the first "cafeteria" launched in 1893 by W.H. Dittmer. Some hotels, such as the Sherman House in Chicago, opened "coffee shops," a concept that soon became ubiquitous in hotels. But at the time, they were considered very controversial. 100th

Tales of a Tragic Night at Sea
by Len Vermillion

While special Senate investigation hearings have become more commonplace in modern times — think of the recent baseball steroids hearings — in the days before electronic mass media, such hearings were reserved for only truly monumental events. In 1912, one such event took place — a tragedy that still haunts legions of people obsessed with finding out what happened to cause such despair — the sinking of the *R.M.S. Titanic*.

When the supposedly unsinkable ocean liner sank into the icy waters of the North Atlantic, the United States Senate immediately demanded to know the truth behind what caused the loss of more than two-thirds of the 2,223 people aboard. On April 19, just four days after the disaster, a special subcommittee of the Senate Commerce Committee, chaired by Senator William Alden Smith, convened a panel investigation in the ornate East Room of New York City's Waldorf=Astoria hotel. Eventually, the 17 days of eyewitness testimony would be completed at the newly built caucus room of the Russell Senate Office Building in Washington, D.C., but it was at the Waldorf where America got its first accounts of the traumatic stories from that infamous night on the sea.

One day after the survivors of the *Titanic* had finally stepped ashore in New York Harbor. Smith rushed with his colleagues from Washington to hear the eyewitness accounts of 82 survivors in an attempt to get to the bottom of what went wrong. The hearings began the next day while still in New York to ensure that the British shipping officials and crew aboard the vessel couldn't leave the country before questioning.

The East Room was jammed with curious and concerned citizens, as well as countless reporters armed with pens and notepads. The accounts of the eye-witnesses have formed the fabric of how the people of the times and future generations transcribed the harrowing tales of both the survivors and the dead. The survivors testified about ice warnings that were ignored, the inadequate number of lifeboats, the ship's speed, the failure of nearby ships to respond to the ship's distress calls, and the varying treatment of passengers of different classes. ●

THE NEW YORK HERALD.

THE TITANIC SINKS WITH 1,800 ON BOARD; ONLY 675, MOSTLY WOMEN AND CHILDREN, SAVED

MOST APPALLING DISASTER IN MARINE HISTORY OCCURS WHEN WORLD'S LARGEST STEAMSHIP STRIKES GIGANTIC ICEBERG AT NIGHT

1910
● **AAA Meets at the Willard**
At a February meeting at the Willard Hotel in Washington, D.C., the American Automobile Association (AAA) lobbied the government for passage of the Federal Registration Bill, which eliminated state barriers to interstate travel.

1916
● **U.S. Purchases Virgin Islands**
On August 4, the United States purchased what is now the U.S. Virgin Islands from Denmark. The territory provided prime real estate and easier entry into a new tropical market for hotels.

1918
● **Spanish Flu Affects Business**
Following World War I, the nation was struck by an influenza pandemic called "Spanish Flu." Fear of the disease paralyzed the public as 40 million people worldwide died. Like many service industries, the hospitality sector suffered lowered demand as people avoided public gathering spots and travel.

1919
● **Prohibition Passes**
Passage of the Federal Volstead Act forced hoteliers to band together to fight the threat to their businesses. They cited the protection of interstate commerce as their basis for argument.

In 1928, developer Harry Wardman opened the iconic Hay-Adams Hotel in Lafayette Square across from the White House.

1920-1929

The Golden Age of Grand Hotels

by Robert Allegrini

In many ways, the Roaring Twenties constituted a golden age for American hotels. Fueled initially by a surging economy, along with the expansion of rail and automobile transportation, this period gave birth to many of the most venerable properties in the pantheon of the nation's lodgings. With increases in workers' leisure time and an unbridled sense of optimism, these impressive, opulent properties drew guests from across the globe. These included luxurious urban palace hotels such as New York's Sherry-Netherland and Lexington; Washington, D.C.'s, Willard and Mayflower; Chicago's Drake, Stevens, and current Palmer House. Other hotels that epitomize this era include the Los Angeles Biltmore, Beverly Wilshire and Mark Hopkins, as well as several of the nation's most famous resorts, including the Arizona Biltmore, the Breakers Hotel in Palm Beach, and the Miami Biltmore in Coral Gables, Florida.

On the opposite end of the spectrum, the 1920s also witnessed the rapid proliferation of smaller motor hotels. The fast growth of motels from the 1920s to the onset of World War II was nearly continuous. Not even the Great Depression could halt their construction as Americans had taken to the roads with gusto. In 1919, there were 6.7 million cars in the United States, but between 1920 and 1929 the number had swollen to 27 million. During that same period, an additional 483,000 miles of roads were built across the country, and motels quickly sprang up next to them, giving rise to an iconic American structure. The attraction of these facilities for motorists was great as the motels offered convenient locations, easy parking, and low prices.

The increase in automobiles, roads, and railway connections also contributed to the enhanced popularity of a range of resort destinations. These included a number of large hotels situated in a variety of areas — from the Catskill Mountains located in New York State, to the Pocono Mountains in Pennsylvania — to the beach resorts of South Florida. As the building of hotels reached an all time peak in the 1920s, occupancy through the decade ran a staggering 85 percent.

This decade constituted an era when several of the grandest names in the history of the 20th century American hospitality industry were all active in some way. E.M Statler continued to expand his empire until his death in 1928. In 1923, he opened his second Buffalo, New York, hotel and then introduced the legendary Detroit Statler in 1927. Meanwhile, John McEntee Bowman spent the 1920s building his Biltmore chain across the nation as well as in Cuba, before his untimely death at age 56 in 1931. In Texas, a young Conrad Hilton spent the 1920s building and buying hotels throughout the state. Meanwhile, half a continent away, J. Willard Marriott was opening his first Hot Shoppe, which was the precursor of his hotel empire that would be based in Washington, D.C., in 1927.

Similarly, the period of the 1920s was an age when legendary giants in the history of AHA held major posts. In 1923, Frank Dudley became AHA's

In the 1920s, automobile travel became more popular, contributing to increased interest in resort destinatons.

The **first collegiate program** in hotel and restaurant management is initiated at **Cornell University.**

The **Millennium Biltmore Hotel** opens in downtown Los Angeles, as the largest hotel **west of Chicago.**

The **Sir Walter Raleigh Hotel** is constructed. It is currently the **oldest surviving hotel building** in Raleigh , North Carolina.

1920   1921   1922   1923   1924

president. At the time, he was head of the largest hotel chain in the country, United Hotels, and his visionary leadership helped to professionalize the association in new ways. The association opened an office in Washington, D.C., and hired a prominent California hotelier, John F. Shea, as executive secretary. For the first time, the association became involved in areas such as public information, image building, vocational training, code of ethics, telephone service, fire prevention, insurance rates, copyright music licensing fees, and uniform accounting systems — an issue that was important to hoteliers in the 1920s.

From Dudley, the association passed into the hands of Tom Green, "the Father of the Federation," who held the reigns of AHA for the next 14 years. He embraced Dudley's mission and continued to transform the organization from a debating society with grandiose ideas (but little ability to put these ideas into practice), into a federation of state, regional, and provincial organizations. As a hotelier, Green owned the elite Woodward Hotel in New York City and was head of the New York City Hotel Association. As president of the organization, Green succeeded in enhancing the association on a number of different levels.

In the world of education, hospitality was a subject that occupied the attention of several leading figures of AHA in the early 1920s. In June 1920, the Lewis Hotel Training School in Washington, D.C., graduated twenty-five students, publicizing the group as the "first class in the United States to graduate from a recognized hotel school." But John Howie of the Hotel Touraine in Buffalo, along with Frank Dudley, proposed a college program for training in hotel management. They and others envisioned the hotel school graduate as a man or woman of culture and broad learning, not a narrowly trained technician. But getting such a curriculum into state universities would not be easy. The hoteliers turned to Cornell University, which had been offering courses in food preparation and service to individuals interested in hotel work through the School of Home Economics in the College of Agriculture since before World War I. Howie and Dudley convinced the leadership of Cornell that

Outside the Hotel McCurdy in Evansville, Illinois, during the 1926 convention of the Hotel Men's Mutual Benefit Association.

- The **first roadside motel** opens in San Luis Obispo, Calif.

- The first **Howard Johnson's** opens as an apothecary **in Wollaston, Mass.**

- The **massive 3,000-room Stevens** (now the Hilton) opens in Chicago as **the largest hotel in the world**, featuring the latest innovations and design elements.

- Opening of the hotel **George V**.

- The **Hotel Pierre** opened in New York City. It was managed by **Charles Pierre**, who was a famous London restaurateur.

- In Phoenix, Arizona, the iconic **Arizona Biltmore** opens its doors to guests.

- The first airport hotel, The Oakland Airport Inn, opens in California.

| 1925 | 1926 | 1927 | 1928 | 1929 |

the quality of the hospitality industry would improve if its management was taught to apply scientific principles of sanitation, efficiency, and consumer economics. Their lobbying came to fruition in 1922 when the first collegiate courses in hotel administration began at Cornell. Thus, hospitality began the march from a trade learned

profits had come mainly from the sale of liquor he never found it necessary to set room rates "scientifically."

That all changed with the onset of Prohibition. Overnight hoteliers were deprived of liquor revenue, and the institution of the speakeasy replaced that of the hotel bar. AHA did not

A group of hotel magnates gathered for a banquet at The Broadmoor as guests of Spencer Penrose, who financed construction of the Colorado resort.

The Broadmoor began as a small hotel and casino in the 1800s. It became a renowned resort in 1918.

by apprenticeship into a profession learned in the classroom.

While the 1920s was surely an era of great progress for many facets of hospitality, the decade was not without its problems for the industry. The first and foremost was the enactment of the 18th Amendment, which made Prohibition the law of the land. Before the onset of the World War I, many hoteliers' profits came largely from the sale of alcohol. E.M. Statler illustrated this point in an article in the *New York Hotel Review* in October 1920, when he explained that he had typically sold "a few rooms, some food, and lots of booze." Because

take firm action at the time to prevent Prohibition, and according to historian Doris King, "the American hotelmen seemingly accepted the 18th Amendment in 1920 as the will of the people and beyond question." One hotelier speaking at a convention in Texas even referred to Prohibition as "something of a blessing," because it cut down on noise and damage to property caused by inebriated guests. Of course, many hotels adapted to Prohibition by housing speakeasies on their premises. Some hotels compensated for the loss of alcohol revenue by the great increase in occupancy that occurred in the 1920s, spurred by in-

Tom Green:
'Mr. AHA'

by Matt Brinn

Prior to the nationwide consolidation of hotel management, operating a hotel could potentially be a very dangerous business. Competition was fierce, employees were sometimes unreliable, and the transient nature of the travel world was not always safe. In its early years, the mission of the American Hotel Association, as written in its constitution, was "... protection against deadbeats, check forgers, dishonest and undesirable employees, and crooks of all descriptions."

In the 1920s, AHA was run by eight executive board members, the most prominent of whom was Thomas Dismukes Green, the owner of the Woodward Hotel in New York City. By the end of World War I, AHA had expanded quite a bit beyond its original mission as a guardian against deadbeat guests. In addition to offering protection to hoteliers nationwide, it also organized legislative endeavors, promotional campaigns, and various educational programs.

At the time, Green was considered to be one of the most well-spoken hoteliers in the industry. He has been described as stubborn and known to have changed his mind on more than one occasion. In 1924, Green vehemently opposed the consolidation of his organization into a federation. The very next year, he was elected president of the organization and played a key role in convincing each state to join the federation.

The restructuring of AHA in the mid-1920s took a heavy toll on the organization's profitability. Revenue was so dismal that several key executives were forced to pay off debts with their own money. Green, who had already made his fortune at the Woodward Hotel, worked as president of AHA without pay for two years before being forced to sustain the organization using his own fortune.

Refusing to back down when faced with a challenge, Green risked it all in 1927 when he bought a 99-year lease on *Hotel Red Book*, a popular hotel guide of the time. The gamble paid off and it turned out to be a very lucrative purchase, providing substantial revenue and paying almost every AHA salary for nearly two decades.

They called him "Mr. AHA" during his tenure, and when Green stepped down in 1940, AHA had grown into an extremely profitable and nationally recognized institution. As president, he had traveled across the nation convincing hoteliers to join him one by one. When times were tough, he sacrificed his pay and his fortune to keep the organization together, and when he saved AHA by purchasing *Hotel Red Book*, he quickly sealed his fate as one of the most important figures in the 100-year history of the association. ●

Other Notables

● **L.G. Treadway**
In the 1920s, Treadway Inns were remarkably different when compared to other rival hotel chains. Instead of standardizing architecture and furniture, Treadway built each inn according to a unique theme, while ensuring his guests memorable meals and décor.

● **Peter Schmidt**
Schmidt helped form Western Hotels, which grew exponentially and over several decades transformed into the modern Westin Hotels & Resorts.

creased travel opportunities and a soaring economy.

Other problems for the industry in the 1920s centered on labor issues. Due to unemployment suffered by bartenders in the wake of Prohibition, the American Federation of Labor's Hotel and Restaurant Employees Union lost thousands of members between 1917 and 1925. However,

securing a larger supply of immigrant workers, but in the wake of the Bolshevik revolution and subsequent Red Scare, every immigrant was made suspect. In deference to the public's fear of foreigners in this era, hotel associations sometimes set up their own employment agencies for the purpose of screening job applicants according to their political notions. It became quite fashionable

Members of AHA gathered at the Sherman House in Chicago in 1925 for the opening of the Bal Tabarin Room, which became renowned as a place for music and entertainment.

this and other unions made significant gains in the post-World War I era. Hugo Ernst, the most aggressive leader within the American Federation of Labor group, sought to rebuild his organization around a large group of skilled cooks. Incensed because he believed hotel owners preferred non-union European immigrant workers and Mexicans to American citizens who belonged to unions, Ernst called for an all-out war against hotels. Hotelmen indeed were interested in

for hotel operators to require workers to attend classes in English and "Americanism."

In addition, one of the consistent calls championed by the labor unions in their negotiations with hotels during this period was for a six-day work-week and an eight-hour workday. One of the first hotel companies to capitulate to this demand was the Boomer-Dupont Company, headed by Lucius Boomer, who heralded a trend

The Industry's First 'Golden Age'

by Marla Cimini

In the United States, the decade commonly known as the "Roaring Twenties," was characterized by a major national economic upswing. This widespread prosperity was also widely enjoyed throughout the hospitality industry.

During this era of the first "hotel boom," the thriving economy saw hotel enhancements across a sweeping spectrum, from the brand new, sizeable, upscale resorts — to the motor inns multiplying along the nation's highways.

For the first time, luxurious vacation properties were constructed in the mountains, initially attracting wealthy patrons with the funds to support such lavish getaways. East Coast mountain resorts in the Catskills region, located in New York State outside of Manhattan, as well as in the Pocono Mountains, north of Philadelphia, Pennsylvania, surged in popularity as the country's enhanced railroad transportation allowed easy access to these areas, which were previously undeveloped and difficult to reach. In addition, with the automobile quickly becoming a common mode of transportation, at least among the well-healed crowd, these large resorts saw an influx of enthusiastic guests.

Meanwhile, the smaller motor inns also made a significant impact on the flourishing hotel industry. Filling a serious need for those travelers driving to their destinations, these motor hotels, (or motels, as they became known), quickly became a phenomenon, dotting the newly paved roads from New York to California. Crossing all demographics, these nondescript motels welcomed guests with the promise of a clean room and a convenient location.

New technologies were also impressing guests on all levels. During the 1920s major improvements were made inside guestrooms as well. None was more noticeable to guests than the innovative ventilation systems that became more common during this decade. They pumped fresh, clean air into hotel guestrooms, while non-slamming hinges were installed on doors to keep the hallways peaceful and guests well heeled. ●

1921
● **NCR** (National Cash Register Company) introduced an innovative **posting machine** that was first installed at the 2,000-room **Pennsylvania Hotel** in New York City.

1926
● President **Calvin Coolidge** signed a bill in Washington, D.C., to create the **American Highway System**.

1927
● Boston's **Hotel Statler** was the first hotel to offer **radio reception** in guestrooms.

● In California, **The Huntington Hotel** installed the first **Olympic-size hotel swimming pool**.

1928
● Another invention from **NCR** was introduced to the hotel world, becoming the first solution to enhance operations by mechanizing **back-office accounting**.

1929
● The **Western Hotel** chain (now Westin) was created, with 17 properties in the Pacific Northwest. It became the **first management company** in the United States.

by giving his workers "one day of rest in seven," but required them to study "Americanism" and wear red, white, and blue ribbons.

Despite these issues, the 1920s will be best remembered as a period when the grandest of grand hotels were in style. Their unique construction reflected the strength and vitality of an America that had emerged from World War I as the world's new economic superpower.

would wear sophisticated evening gowns and sparkling jewelry, and their gentlemen counterparts wore white ties and top hats. During the 1920s, many wealthy guests simply never checked out of their accommodations. Instead, they made luxury hotel suites their permanent residence for years at a time.

Hotels played center stage in this glamorous era. It seems only natural that the backdrop for scenes in F. Scott Fitzgerald's masterpiece *The Great Gatsby*, which defined the 1920s more than any other work of literature, was New York's elegant Plaza Hotel.

Members of AHA's Executive Council at the Botsford Tavern in Clarenceville, Michigan, as guests of Henry Ford.

It was an age not only of colorful hotel guests, but of flamboyant hotel hosts as well. Men such as the famous Oscar Tschirky, known across the nation as "Oscar of the Waldorf" presided over the Waldorf=Astoria's banquets and restaurants. Considered the "face of the hotel," Oscar greeted kings and presidents when he wasn't busy inventing Waldorf Salad or popularizing Thousand Island dressing.

The patrons of the grand hotels of the time could be expected to arrive elegantly clad and coiffed, often accompanied by a personal maid or valet and several steamer trunks. Many of the hotels of the period were constructed with an arcade level below the lobby with service providers such as hairdressers, barbers, and cobblers. When guests emerged for dinner, ladies more often than not

The mentality in vogue at the time was one of elegance, fun, and congeniality. However, this was all about to soon change. Not far into the future, the boom times of the decade would end abruptly with the stock market crash of October 1929, sending the United States falling into the Great Depression. **100**ᵗʰ

And the Winner Is ...

by Len Vermillion

The modern day presentation of the Academy Awards is a gala event, viewed by millions of people across the world on television. But it wasn't always that way. On a spring evening in Hollywood's Roosevelt Hotel, the Oscars, as they are affectionately known, began with little fanfare and little intrigue. In fact, the first Academy Awards went practically unnoticed by the general public.

On May 16, 1929, fewer than 250 people gathered in the hotel's Blossom Room for a black-tie dinner and awards ceremony. And they arrived already knowing who the winners would be.

They began the evening with a dinner of Filet of Sole Saute au Buerre and Half-Broiled Chicken on Toast. Then, Douglas Fairbanks, the president of the Academy of Motion Picture Arts and Sciences, which was established less than two years earlier, stood up and gave a speech. With the help of William C. deMille, he called the winners up to the head table and handed them the awards they'd won.

What was drastically different from today's ceremony is that three months earlier, the Academy had already announced the winners to the press. Since the eligibility was from August 1, 1927 to July 31, 1928, voting was completed much earlier than the awards ceremony.

Who won? The first Oscar was awarded to Emil Jannings for Best Actor for his roles in *The Last Command* and *The Way of All Flesh*. Janning wasn't even at the ceremony. He decided to go back to his native Germany before the ceremony so he was handed the award before he left for his trip.

Other winners that year included *Wings*, for Picture (Production); *Sunrise: A Song of Two Humans*, Picture (Unique and Artistic Production); Janet Gaynor, Actress (*Seventh Heaven*; *Street Angel*; *Sunrise*); and both Frank Borzage (*Seventh Heaven*) and Lewis Milestone (*Two Arabian Knights*) for Director.

There is one thing that hasn't changed over the years. The Oscar statuette, which was sculpted by George Stanley, was almost exactly the same then as it is today. ●

1920

● The Algonquin Roundtable Begins
Throughout the '20s and '30s many of the best-known writers, journalists, and artists in New York City met at an informal lunch gathering on weekdays at The Algonquin Hotel. Among the regulars were Dorothy Parker, Alexander Woollcott, Heywood Broun, Robert Sherwood, George S. Kaufman, Franklin P. Adams, Marc Connelly, Harold Ross, Harpo Marx, and Russell Crouse.

1923

● The Charleston Becomes Popular
The Charleston became popular after it was performed in the Broadway musical, *Runnin' Wild*. Dancers performed the moves to the song of the same name, which was sung by James P. Johnson. Soon ballrooms in hotels across the country were hosting ragtime jazz bands so guests could do the dance.

1924

● The Prince of Wales At The Drake
Known mostly as the home of the Amos 'n' Andy radio show, The Drake Hotel hosted a special guest when His Royal Highness, the Prince of Wales, chose to stay at the hotel during his visit to Chicago. The visit marked the start of an 84-year tradition as the home of the royal family during visits to the city.

In the 1930s, The Driskill hotel in Austin, Texas, served as a centerpiece of the city's entertainment venues.

1930-1939

Triumph in the Face of Adversity

by Robert Allegrini

Like most other segments of the nation's economy, it was not long into the 1930s before the lodging industry began to feel the pain of the Great Depression. However, a number of construction developments were already underway, so many of the grandiose hotel projects that had begun in the 1920s were fortunately still able to come to fruition in the early '30s. Among these projects were the venerable Pierre Hotel in New York, as well as another hotel that was to subsequently earn the moniker of "the greatest of them all" — the new Waldorf=Astoria Hotel, which opened to the public on September 30, 1931.

35

The opening of properties such as the Pierre and the Waldorf=Astoria gives lie to the myth that the decade was one long soup line of misery. Actually, much of the glamour and high style that characterized hotels in the good times of the 1920s contin-

By 1932, nearly three-quarters of the nation's hotels were in trouble. At the AHA convention in Memphis in October of that year, the association's past president Frank Dudley stated, "The hotel industry apparently has suffered equally, and perhaps greater, than any other industry as the result of the Depression ... from the best records obtainable in the United States, there are 70 percent of the important hotels of the country that are either in the hands of receivers, bondholder committees, mortgagees in possession, or are in the process of reorganization."

Hoteliers gathered at The Peabody hotel in Memphis in 1932 for the annual AHA convention.

ued throughout the 1930s, although, with fewer people employed, there were clearly far fewer guests in a position to take advantage of all that the urban grand hotels and their resort counterparts had to offer. In fact, during this time occupancy rates at hotels tumbled to their lowest point in recorded history, coming in at a dismal 51 percent.

These conditions were accentuated by two factors. First, Prohibition had deprived hotels of a profitable and normally legitimate segment of the innkeeping business. Second, as the Depression widened, hotel owners (and especially those placed in charge by banks, mortgage companies, insurance companies, and bondholder committees) were panicked into unethical and harmful practices. This included selling food and rooms at any price in order to maintain some kind of cash flow, however inadequate.

● **The Waldorf=Astoria** in New York City moves to its 42-story, 2,200-room current location, at the time considered the **largest hotel in the world.**

● Due to the **Great Depression,** hotels post the **lowest average occupancy rate** on record, **51 percent.** New construction grinds to a halt.

● **Lyndon B. Johnson** meets his future wife, **Lady Bird,** for their first date in **The Driskill** dining room.

1930   1931   1932   1933   1934

At the Memphis Convention, Ben Hoag of Marietta, Ohio, made an urgent plea for "hotelmen" to stop these disastrous practices. He reported that city hotels were selling rooms with bathrooms for $3 per day, while giving free garage parking, free breakfasts and, sometimes, free laundry. He stated he knew of hotels charging only 75 to 95 cents for complete meals. "Gentlemen, for God's sake, let us do something," he concluded.

Conrad Hilton, who was then president of the Texas Hotel Association, echoed Hoag's concern when he pleaded, "Can't we compete in serving the guest and not in killing each other?" Regrettably, in most cases during the Great Depression the answer was simply "no," as evidenced by the fact that the percentage of American hotels that went into some form of receivership between 1929 and 1936 eventually climbed to an astounding 88 percent.

AHA was simultaneously suffering the same fate as its member hotels. In 1933, the association reported about $20,000 in uncollected dues — a considerable sum for the era. In order to bridge the revenue gap, President Thomas Dismukes Green and Emerson Owen, manager of the *Hotel Red Book*, created a sustaining membership program that provided a range of individual services to sustaining hotels on the basis of 100 rooms for $25. To further augment revenues, it was proposed to invite suppliers to become allied members.

These plans, designed as emergency measures, were instrumental in carrying the association through the dark days of the Depression. Their major contribution to history, however, was that they established a direct relationship between hotels and AHA for the first time and created the Allied Membership Division, which continues to make valuable contributions to the association to this day.

With the boom in travel that sustained hotels through the "dry" 1920s over, AHA began to take a second look at how Prohibition was denying the hospitality industry a valuable source of much needed revenue. Consequently, early in 1932, the executive council of the association unanimously resolved that the time

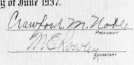

AHA President Thomas Green was given a life membership to the Hotel Greeters of America.

To help build needed revenue during the Great Depression, suppliers joined AHA as Allied Members.

● Membership in the **Waiters and Bartenders National Union**, which encompasses hotel employees, **exceeds 200,000.**

● **Quality Courts United,** later **Choice Hotels International,** is formed by seven motel operators as a **nonprofit referral system.**

935   1936   1937   1938   1939

had come to support repeal of the 18th Amendment. To get the job done, President Green turned to his friend Arthur L. Race of the Copley Plaza in Boston.

Race immersed himself in the issue, devoting his energy almost full time to the cause for the next 18 months. He set up a National Prohibition Committee supported by parallel chairmen and committees in each state. These committees worked feverishly for the election of "wet" candidates as the anti-Prohibition candidates were known. They engineered a string of underdog victories for "wet" congressional and gubernatorial candidates across the country.

Taking notice of the shifting political landscape, Franklin Roosevelt, who had wooed the dry vote for some time, came forward on a platform at the 1932 Democratic Convention that favored the outright repeal of the 18th Amendment. With his election, the die was cast and Prohibition was officially repealed on December 5, 1933. This victory clearly marked the most effective incursion of AHA in the legislative arena up to that time. It is considered to be one of the most successful on a specific issue ever undertaken by the association.

The view of Manhattan from the roof of the newly built (and modern-day site) of the Waldorf=Astoria.

The return of the free flow of alcohol in hotels set the stage for one of the greatest hospitality innovations of the 1930s — the supper club. It is no mere coincidence that many of the grandest supper clubs in the nation opened in the mid-1930s in the immediate aftermath of Prohibition. These clubs included such legendary names as The Persian Room at The Plaza, The Empire Room at The Palmer House, The Biltmore Bowl at the Los Angeles Biltmore, and The Blue Room at The Roosevelt in New Orleans. Impressively appointed and often featuring extensive menus and big name musical entertainment, the hotel supper clubs of the 1930s were venues where the Depression could be forgotten. They became the places to go for a romantic and sophisticated night out. Guests attired in their formal best could sip champagne cocktails, watch floor shows, and dance to the big bands that were popular in the era.

Interestingly, supper clubs were not the only culinary venues that proliferated in the 1930s. Even as the Depression deepened, the number of full-fledged restaurants continued to increase from 134,293 in 1929 to 169,792 in 1939 — largely as the result of Prohibition's demise. It was an era of themed restaurants with imaginative décor that mimicked venues such as ships, castles, or European courtyards. Hotel restaurants followed this trend and a few of these themed restaurants, such as The Drake hotel's nautically inspired Cape Cod Room, opened in 1933. They have managed to survive until this day. What did not survive the 1930s,

Earnest Henderson & Robert Moore: Ingenuity and Thrift

by Jay Krupp

Ernest Henderson (shown above) and Robert Moore, co-founders of the Sheraton Corporation, transformed the hospitality industry in the 1930s. Who could have guessed that a small business, whose namesake was inspired by an old broken sign emblazoned with the words "Sheraton Hotel," would evolve into a multinational conglomerate?

Henderson and Moore, Harvard classmates in the early 20th century, tried many businesses before finding success with hotels. From assembling Model-T cars to importing German shepherd dogs, they tried almost everything before settling on hospitality. After the stock market crashed, they found an opportunity and entered the securities business. Taking highly unorthodox approaches with investments and setting up one of the first mutual funds in the nation eventually led them to the hotel industry. They purchased additional investment companies and focused on the real estate value of hotels. Buying poorly performing or foreclosed hotels and turning them around at a considerable profit became their recipe for success. Real estate investments remained part of their portfolio up until Henderson's death in 1967.

In 1937, Henderson and Moore acquired the Stonehaven Hotel in Springfield, Massachusetts. This was the first of four hotels they would purchase in Massachusetts over a two-year period. With a well-structured management approach, they found they could increase their revenue. It was this model that bore the Sheraton Corporation. Over the next decade they expanded their holdings and in 1945 became the first hotel chain to be listed on the New York Stock Exchange.

Being masterful with finances, Henderson took advantage of federal depreciation allowances to reduce taxable income. This provided money for further expansion, keeping profits low but sending the assets soaring high. Using their experience and thriftiness, they expanded the Sheraton name, while minimizing corporate expenditures by taking on the management of hotels built by others.

Sheraton expanded internationally to Canada in 1949 with the purchase of two Canadian hotel chains. The company continued its expansion in the United States to include motor inns and resorts in Hawaii. In 1968, the conglomerate ITT purchased the chain of hotels, changing the name to ITT Sheraton. The company's international growth continued and, in 1998, Starwood Hotels and Resorts Worldwide acquired the Sheraton brand. ●

Other Notables

● **J.F. Patterson and A.J. Mckay**
Shortly after Quality Courts United was formed Patterson and Mckay became its president and secretary. After organizing the corporation against negative propaganda spread by J. Edgar Hoover, they grew Quality Courts United into one of the largest motel franchises in the world.

however, were many of the menu items that were popular at the time. A look at one luxury hotel restaurant menu from the period revealed such items as "Boned Pigs Feet in Jelly," "Tongue Sandwiches," "Sardine Sandwiches," "Mutton Chops," "Welsh Rarebit," "Clear Green Turtle Soup," and "Braised Larded Calf's Sweetbreads." Needless to say, culinary tastes greatly changed during the ensuing decades.

variety and color. For those who still had money, the benefit of the Depression was that almost everything was made affordable, including the most fabulous and outrageous of parties.

During this era of "haves" and "have nots," many hotels adopted the mantra of "Black Tie, Front Door; No Tie, Back Door!" That is not to say, however, that hotels did not have a heart during the Depression. Several

Members of the International Hotel Alliance gathered at the Waldorf=Astoria in 1934.

Paradoxically, it was the Great Depression that also made the 1930s an era of some of the most imaginative and extravagant hotel parties to date. It was a time for escapism and no venue could make illusions seem so real or so complete as the grand hotel where "anything was possible." Throughout the 1930s, ballrooms were transformed for theme parties with the aid of elaborate props that often included live animals, trees, birds, cabanas, painted backdrops, and costumed waiters, in addition to the ever present extravagant use of flowers of practically every known

hotels such as the Mayflower in Washington, D.C., set up canteens at their own expense to feed the local down and out. The coming of President Roosevelt's New Deal would help many of those downtrodden recover, but for AHA it was to become a source of great consternation.

The frustration for AHA with regard to the New Deal centered largely on the newly created National Recovery Administration (NRA). The NRA was charged with negotiating codes of fair practices with specific industries, which were intended to

Depression Paralyzes the Industry

by Marla Cimini

As the Great Depression took a firm grasp of the United States' economy, the optimism of 1920s was quickly replaced with the gloom of the 1930s. Like the rest of the country, hotel owners during this era were hesitant to innovate, and focused more on the survival of their businesses than embracing new products or services. The hospitality industry in the 1930s saw a drastic drop in hotel occupancy, which led to the closing of some hotels and an abrupt end to the wave of luxury property construction across the United States.

Not surprisingly, the growth rate of U.S. patent applications by companies was considerably lower during the 1930s than in the preceding decade. However, one major technological advancement during this volatile decade stemmed from the world of telecommunications. In 1938, AT&T encouraged the use of telephones in individual guestrooms by offering hotels a commission on long distance calls made by their guests.

In the late 1930s, several changes occurred as a result of President Franklin Roosevelt's implementation of the New Deal programs, some of which eventually assisted those most affected by the Depression, and helped spark a resurgence in the travel world.

The end of the decade was marked by a major revival in the hospitality industry, as it once again began to flourish. So much, in fact, that in 1939, the American Hotel Association decided to host a celebration, and declared June 11-17 of that year National Hotel Week. Hotels during this time numbered approximately 20,000, and featured a total of 1,750,000 guestrooms. By the end of the 1930s, people were certainly traveling again, and beginning to see signs of new innovations slowly appearing in hotels, such as the air conditioning that was starting to be installed in some of the finest properties across the nation. ●

1934

● In keeping with its founder's ideals of seeking new innovations for his hotels, the **Hotel Statler in Detroit, Michigan,** was the first hotel in the United States to take advantage of a young technology that **allowed it to offer central air conditioning in its property.** It was an attactive luxury for guests, most of whom had never experienced it before.

1935

● **George and Ladislo Biro invented the ball point pen.** Hoteliers discovered that offering pens to guests as souveniers, as well as for functional uses, became a surprisingly popular amenity.

1937

● **Chester F. Carlson invented the photocopy machine** (although it didn't become commercially available until the 1950s.)

1939

● **The first flight was made by a jet airplane.** The flight, and ensuing airline industry, opened up an efficient way for people to travel around the world. Eventually, airline travel significantly aided the growth of the hospitality and tourism industry by allowing more Americans to travel to distant and exotic locales that were not previously available to them.

reduce "destructive competition," and to help workers by setting minimum wages and maximum hours.

This proved to be an impossible task with regard to the hospitality industry. The initial code proposed by AHA was turned down by the NRA. Eventually, a code was developed, primarily by NRA staff, which was never agreed to by AHA. This code was virtually impossible to live by. Discussion of its implications was to dominate the 1934 AHA convention which, as a result of this issue, drew the largest number of delegates ever to have attended such a gathering.

A view of the grand lobby of The Driskill in the 1930s.

All of the delegates hoped for some solution that encompassed rewriting a more equitable code. Many sought relief from threats of reprisals from the NRA for non-compliance. There is little doubt their consternation was justified. After all, how could hotels, particularly smaller properties in receivership or on the brink of bankruptcy, be able to raise wages, shorten hours, and hire more employees when they couldn't even pay their taxes?

In the end, a resolution was passed that since the hotels of the United States could not comply with the NRA code, the president of AHA was authorized to appoint a special committee to meet with President Roosevelt for the purpose of securing relief. Lobbying with administration officials ensued over the next several months and, according to a report made by President Green to the AHA Executive Council on June 1, 1935, the hotels were just on the verge of being granted an exemption from NRA codes when the Supreme Court rendered its historic decision ruling the entire NRA as being unconstitutional. "We were just on the verge of victory when the Supreme Court stepped in and grabbed all the glory," lamented Green. But the AHA president was also sage enough to realize that the Prohibition fight of 1932-1933 and the NRA fight of 1933-1934 did a great deal to unify AHA. To quote Green, "As a result of these two major campaigns, our association has been welded into an efficient fighting force and we are recognized today as never before as an effective instrument for forwarding our program."

While the 1930s was a decade of hardship for the industry, it was also a decade which produced circumstances and issues that compelled AHA to take actions in terms of its structure and agenda, which are still yielding benefits today. Furthermore, the Great Depression had taught hoteliers the discipline of tighter budgetary controls, better cost accounting methods, sounder financing arrangements, and an awareness of the dangers of indiscriminate price cutting. In that way, the most had been made of a very difficult decade for the lodging industry. **100th**

Big Bands Go Remote

by Len Vermillion

Rudy Vallée's Orchestra. Will Osbourne's Dance Band. Ben Bernie. These were just some of the famous big band leaders of the times that were featured on Big Band Remote, a remote radio broadcast that got its start in the 1930s and remained popular throughout the 1940s.

While a nation of listeners thumped their feet in time to the music and danced around their own living rooms, live audiences danced the night away to the big band sounds at some of the finest hotels around. Ballrooms of hotels in cities such as New York, Los Angeles, Philadelphia, San Francisco, and Chicago, became household names as they hosted the broadcasts.

Ben Bernie was heard during weekly remotes from the Roosevelt Hotel in Manhattan. Other big band big names of the era performed live at hotels. Artie Shaw broadcast from the Rose Room in Boston's Ritz-Carlton. However, The Blue Room of New York's Hotel Lincoln was the location of Shaw's only regular radio series as headliner. He broadcast on CBS from 1938 until 1939.

Eventually, names such as Glenn Miller, Duke Ellington, Count Bassie, and Shep Fields, who performed regularly at the Palmer House in Chicago, were into the act.

The broadcasts actually originated in 1923 when listeners could tune into The Waldorf=Astoria Orchestra, and a year later when The Oriole Orchestra broadcast from Chicago's Edgewater Beach Hotel.

The radio remotes continued throughout World War II, even extending to military bases, and remained popular until the 1950s when the concept gave way to similar broadcasts from jazz clubs as the tastes in popular music began to change. ●

1930

● **The Jazz Scene Centers on the Dunbar**

When it opened in 1928, Hotel Somerville hosted the first NAACP national convention to be held in the western United States. In 1930, its name was changed to the Dunbar, and it immediately became the most prestigious hotel in Los Angeles' African-American community. Throughout the '30s, the hotel became the center of the Central Avenue jazz scene and hosted luminaries such as Duke Ellington, Cab Calloway, Louis Armstrong, Count Bassie, Lionel Hampton, and Lena Horne.

1931

● **Molly Brown Moves into Hotel Barbizon**

She may have gained fame for being an "unsinkable" millionaire on the *Titanic*, but in 1931 Molly Brown took ill and lived her final year in New York's Hotel Barbizon, which had become known as a safe haven for young girls moving to Manhattan.

1933

● **Tesla Resides at the New Yorker**

His name might not be as recognizable as Einstein or Edison, but Nikola Tesla lived the last 10 years of his life (until 1943) in the New Yorker Hotel in room 3327.

Upon his retirement, AHA President Tom Green received a watch from AHA vice presidents at the Olympic Hotel in Seattle, Washington.

1940-1949

Hotels on the Home Front

by Harvey Chipkin

This was a decade when the first half was dominated by a cataclysmic event: World War II. Not surprisingly, its impact on the hotel industry was overwhelming — and complex. While occupancies soared because of governmental activities and other forces, there was tremendous sacrifice as well in the form of high taxes, limited resources, and rationing. Still, the industry and its professional association managed to progress on several fronts — putting hotels in a position to take advantage of the prosperity and pent-up demand for leisure travel that followed the end of the fighting.

With the great demand for hotel rooms and services during the war, it became a common sight to see people sleeping in lobbies because there were no rooms available. The challenge for hotel operators was to operate a capacity business with a greatly depleted staff because of the needs of the armed services. During the war, hotel employees by the thousands went into the military; and hotels by the hundreds were taken over by the government. Rates were frozen in 300 defense areas; occupancy shot up from 64 percent to 93 percent in 1945 — but excess income went into wartime taxes and could not be spent for badly needed equipment.

An early Best Western motel in Arizona.

Still, the relentless trend toward professionalism continued on several fronts: in training of employees, in upgrading the industry association, and in other areas as well. Many observers believe that it took World War II to bring trade associations such as AHA to true professionalism. In 1940, Thomas Green stepped down from the AHA presidency, leaving an impressive legacy. In 14 years, he had rescued the association from bankruptcy, paid off its debts (often with personal funds), acquired the *Hotel Red Book*, originated the Allied Membership category, and created national membership — a direct membership division with such benefits as operational counsel from expert consultants.

Membership in 1940 totaled 5,784, with 600,000 rooms; gross income totaled $123,000, of which only $28,000 came from federation dues.

Released from their longtime "responsibility" to re-elect every year, delegates to the 1940 AHA convention were wildly enthusiastic. They elected Franklin Moore of Pennsylvania to be president — but not until the sixth ballot. Despite Moore's capabilities (Lawson Odde, the second executive vice president of the association, who was responsible for the modernization of membership expansion and financial operations, wrote at a later date: "No man was ever available for a position of leadership who had already held more positions of leadership, dynamic candidates

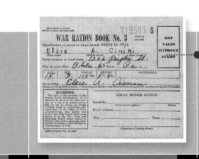

During WW II, **hotels were required to ration products** such as sugar, butter, and tea.

● **Train travel gains popularity** across the United States, opening up a new avenue of travel to remote locations. **Hotels benefit** from the increased traffic.

1940　　　　1941　　　　1942　　　　1943　　　　1944

were all over the place. Memorable debates were conducted." Harold Van Orman of Indiana was elected vice president to serve with Moore. As brilliant speakers, each man was a match for the other as a master of innkeeping lore.

Moore brought in heavyweight industry names to chair committees, including Glen Sherrard of Boston, Frank Andres of New York, Ed Lawless of Chicago, and Dan London of San Francisco. AHA committees soon bloomed with presidents-in-the-making, including John Green (Tom's son) of Williamsburg; J.B. Herndon of Albuquerque; and Harry Gowman of Seattle. AHA's leading women were also on board, including Marge Sefton of the *Hotel Red Book* and Grace Wooley of national membership.

For the association's lobbyists, subjects of concern during this period involved the reduction and repeal of the cabaret tax, unfair competition, and the treatment of tips under various tax laws. Outside counsel was obtained to work to free the industry from government rent controls. On other fronts, activity was rife. Researchers tested fabrics and detergents, soaps, and polishes; Barney Allis of Kansas City agitated for a universal travel card; Frank Andrews

raised a public relations fund so sizable ($81,283 the first year) that, with its separate bank account, it threatened to overwhelm the association (it had more cash.)

Despite bright spots, finding the food to put on menus was frequently a problem because of rationing. Hotels found the problem of rationed sugar one of the most troublesome issues during World War II. In normal times, Americans used about 10 tons of sugar per minute, or 28 million pounds a day. In 1942, much of that sugar was required for the armed forces and the manufacture of explo-

Members of AHA's Resort Hotels Committee gathered in 1947 at the Homestead Hotel in Hot Springs, Virginia.

- **Sheraton** is the first hotel corporation to be listed on the **New York Stock Exchange.**
- **Travelodge** becomes the first economy-lodging corporation.

- **Best Western** is founded by **M.K. Guertin** and 54 friends.

- **Hilton** becomes the first **international** chain with the opening of the **Caribe Hilton** in San Juan, Puerto Rico.

945   1946   1947   1948   1949

47

sives. Sugar hoarding also contributed to the shortage. Consequently, hotels were assigned a 50 percent quota. All hotels were advised to ration sugar to customers immediately. Restaurant operators were ordered to remove sugar bowls from tables and counters and to ration sugar to customers at the rate of one rounded teaspoon for each cup of coffee, bowl of cereal, or fruit portion. Severe penalties were mandated for violators.

Conservation suggestions encouraged saving syrup from canned fruits and using them to sweeten other fruits, puddings, and beverages, and to use sweet-pickle vinegar for preparing mayonnaise and other dressings. Other suggestions included reducing the size of desserts; and promoting the use of honey, pre-sweetened tea, and a sugar substitute, saccharin.

However, there was no rationing when it came to training, as even understaffed hoteliers realized its importance early in the tumultuous decade. In 1940, the Hotel Statler Company was one of the leaders in taking a sympathetic, personal approach to hotel management. According to Statler executives, "just as you couldn't build with weak or misfit

In the 1940s, elevator men, such as these men from the Copley Plaza in Boston, were a common sight at hotels.

timber, no hotel department could operate when the human material was unskilled, unadaptable, or unsuited for the work."

In 1940, there were two important rules to consider in the selection of Statler employees: (1) Draw up a specialization card and gauge an employee by his answers; and (2) Do not hire or retain a shiftless, wrangling, or morally unclean employee. Among the Statler principles in dealing with employees were, "Every man wants a bit of personal attention — a greeting, a gesture of friendliness, or an inquiry about his work. This satisfies a desire to be recognized." Other principles adopted by the company included, "appreciating an expression of sympathy and assistance when sorrow strikes." The Statler hiring process began looking for a worker who "wants words of praise for work well done, who takes satisfaction in having work delegated to them, who wants the opportunity to accomplish results of some importance, and who wants to be proud of his company."

But after the years or rationing and coping, the situation went from paucity to prosperity with the end of the war. Despite dire predictions that the U.S. economy would tailspin into a major economic depression once the economic stimulus of the Great War ended, the nation entered into a period of soaring economic prosperity. Pent-up demand for material goods was released and — even more important for the resort industry — the demand for fun and relaxation was once again satisfied. After experiencing years of the Great Depression

Conrad Hilton: Laying the Foundations

by Melissa Mijares

Conrad Nicholson Hilton, Sr., had been in the hotel business for 20 years when he finally expanded his Texas hotel chain in 1939, buying a property in New Mexico. This leap of a few thousand miles would open the doors for further growth. Just seven years later, in 1946, Hilton founded Hilton Hotel Corporation, the first coast-to-coast hotel chain in the country.

The 1940s were Hilton's "golden age," as he became the owner of the opulent Plaza Hotel in New York City and opened the famous Oak Room. What had once been a bar serving men only re-opened as an exclusive and high-end dining restaurant that seated 112 guests. Offering a stunning view of Central Park, this renowned eatery was a hotspot which guests frequented to "see and be seen."

After Hilton bought the Plaza, he spent the rest of the '40s collecting equally prestigious hotels: the Drake in San Francisco, the Palmer House in Chicago, the Roosevelt in New York City, and, finally, in 1949, he acquired "the crown jewel" of Hilton Hotels, the Waldorf=Astoria. Located in the ritzy Upper East Side of Manhattan, it has been said that Hilton greatly preferred the cozy colonial beauty of the Waldorf=Astoria to any of his other properties.

Hilton was married to socialite and celebrity Zsa Zsa Gabor in 1942, and though the marriage ended in 1946, it contributed to his burgeoning reputation as a wealthy and privileged tycoon.

Despite his life of luxury, Hilton would be best remembered as a dedicated philanthropist. Believing always that charity and good deeds would "bind all men in one great brotherhood," he set up the Conrad N. Hilton Foundation to raise money for humanitarian projects throughout the world. Since then, the Foundation has distributed more than $600 million towards such causes. In 1996, the Conrad N. Hilton Humanitarian prize was created, which honors organizations that are dedicated to charitable efforts.

Over the years, the Hilton name has been linked to gossip — from the media frenzy surrounding his personal life to the escapades of his great-granddaughter, Paris. However, the hotel chain has remained a solid brand recognized worldwide for consistency and quality. ●

Other Notables

● **M.K. Guertin**
On his road trip from California to Tacoma, Washington, hotelier M.K. Guertin recorded the distances between motels, paying special attention to those just a "tank of gas" away from one another, and then published his findings as a guide for road travelers. The motels began recommending one another to guests, and what began simply as a network of informally affiliated establishments became Best Western Hotels.

● **Arthur Landstreet**
A long-time Tennessee hotelier throughout the 1940s, Landstreet would go on to found the Educational Institute, which offers training, certification, and education, in the early 1950s. He was the organization's first president.

and then of the rationing of goods because of the war, Americans finally were able to relax and spend money that the economic boom was putting into their pockets.

The Merry Go Round Bar became a popular feature of the Copley Plaza during the 1940s.

In the second half of the 1940s, highway tourism emerged as an economic force in the United States.

Travel and tourism returned as a popular pastime — with a very large and important difference: the age of the automobile and of super highways was upon us. Americans packed their belongings and their families into the family car and headed for vacations in places that were becoming increasingly accessible by interstate highways. Roadside "tourist courts" and motels flourished along with campsites. For the masses of Americans traveling by car, the grand old resort hotels with their pampered lifestyle were of little interest and, furthermore, were unaffordable. Rapid movement and highway tourism was the new hobby.

Returning soldiers with buying power began to purchase and travel. Motel development flourished. Sunbelt locations became popular for small, "mom and pop" properties. Frequently a couple would build about 20 units and handle virtually all labor and management chores within the family. It seemed like a nice business to own. But those who

thought that owning a motel was a form of semi-retirement were in for a rude awakening. Owners were usually summoned from a deep sleep to handle late check-ins. They also had to be alert to guest couples checking in without luggage, lest their property quickly attain a sordid reputation. Theft was always a possibility. But for those willing to word hard, the rewards could be impressive.

By the late 1940s, AHA commanded the services of two of the best qualified trade association professionals of their time: Charlie Horrworth in the New York office and Bud Ryan in Washington, D.C. Horrworth came to AHA from his job as managing director of the California State Hotel Association. He had learned to sell as an executive in a travel and tourism association, and as a Chautauqua lecturer (in the days when Chautauqua lectures often emerged as the literature of the time.) Horrworth electrified audiences. As Lawson Odde was to say later, "He made the industry proud of itself, and the association aware of its vast potential." The two men were charged with implementing the decisions of some of the giants in hotel operations and association service among them: President Franklin Moore, Harold Van Orman, Glen Sherrard, and Ed Frawley.

Reflecting the dramatic change in public awareness of hotel and restaurant cleanliness, J.A. Jones, vice president and general manager of Chicago's Sherman Hotel, said at the July 22, 1948, meeting of AHA, "We cannot afford to hide behind an apron of apparent cleanliness a bed of bac-

Helping the War Effort

by Marla Cimini

During the first half of the 1940s, World War II consumed much of the country's attention. In addition to the overall concern of the ongoing devastation overseas, the United States government began developing new conservation policies at home to combat the fuel shortages that were impacting the nation.

In direct opposition to the earlier decades, which were marked by the hospitality industry's unprecedented growth and overall lavish excess, the focus of the 1940s was primarily on conservation. In fact, the War Protection Board (WPB) in 1945 issued a "brown-out" order that prohibited some uses of electric lighting. Directly affecting the hotel business was the "Utilities Order U-9," which nearly eliminated outdoor electrical lighting used for advertising and related signage. This order from the government resulted in a number of hotels scaling back considerably on their outside display illumination and decorative marquee lighting.

In 1941, the United States government found additional, more pressing uses for hotels located in Florida. That year, the Army Air Corps took command over Miami Beach, and turned some waterfront hotels into military barracks for servicemen. The picturesque stretch of beachfront properties was transformed into a training ground for troops before they were stationed abroad.

In other cities and towns during the war, it was not uncommon for some of larger hotels throughout the United States to host fundraisers for the war effort, such as Los Angeles' Ambassador Hotel, whose well-known Cocoanut Grove was the site of many gala events designed to support the troops. This hotel's popularity grew, and after the war came to an end, the Cocoanut Grove became a retreat for servicemen and women, along with many Hollywood movie stars.

As the decade continued, Choice Hotels International (then Quality Courts United) clearly saw the importance of assisting guests further by publishing accurate hotel directories, which its began offering in 1941. Over the years, these valuable directories became common and useful tools for travelers across the world.

It was the later 1940s that ushered in several new interesting and much-needed services that eventually grew industrywide. ●

1941
● **Choice** was the first hotel company to **print travel directories**.

1946
● **Westin** introduced **credit cards** for guests.

1947
● **Westin** debuted the first hotel reservation system, **Hoteltype**.

● The **Roosevelt Hotel** in New York City was the first to install **televisions** in all guestrooms.

1948
● **Sheraton** was the first chain to utilize a **telex system** for room reservations.

● **Innovative sanitation** attracted attention: The importance of modern **hotel and restaurant cleanliness** was a central topic within the American Hotel Association.

teria in our food establishments that may cause death by menu."

But another kind of infestation (criminal) helped bring about the first luxury hotel casino to be built on what is today's Las Vegas Strip. The Flamingo, opened by gangster Benjamin (Bugsy) Siegel in December of 1946 was the birth of the Las Vegas that we know today. It was not the first hotel casino. That was the El Rancho Vegas, which opened in 1941 with 63 rooms. Its success spawned the Hotel Last Frontier in 1942.

Following the war, hotels around the nation offered accommodations to GIs, who returned from war with nowhere to go.

But then Siegel moved in on businessman Billy Wilkerson, whose vision it was to design a European style hotel with luxurious rooms, a spa, health club, showroom, golf course, nightclub, and upscale restaurant. Because of wartime costs, however, Wilkerson went into debt and when he looked for new financing, it was Siegel who provided it. Siegel and his partners came to Las Vegas because the city had piqued his interest due to its legalized gambling and its off-track betting. Siegel first purchased the El Cortez on Fremont Street, later selling it at a hefty profit. He used those funds to invest $1 mil-

Quality Courts United's travel guides began in the 1940s, helping travelers find their way around America's highways.

lion in Wilkerson's project, allowing Wilkerson to keep an ownership stake and operational control. Siegel brought in more underworld figures and, despite rising costs (some ironically because of theft), he managed to open The Pink Flamingo Hotel & Casino at the end of 1946 — billing it as the world's most luxurious hotel.

Since World War II diverted technical equipment to more urgent goals, lodging properties could not add to their use of existing technology. During the last half of the 1940s hotels started playing catch-up with the limited choices of previously developed technology The NCR Class 2000 started to be accepted for back-office accounting. It was still decades before the computer revolution really took hold, but with huge pent-up demand, a roaring economy, and millions of soldiers returning from war, circumstances were about to change. **100**[th]

Allies Unite for Peace

by Len Vermillion

Franklin Delano Roosevelt coined the expression "United Nations" in 1939 as a reference to the countries fighting against the Axis powers in World War II. The term was used again in a more official manner in 1942 when 26 nations made the "Declaration by United Nations." They pledged to continue their joint war effort and not to make peace separately. But the UN really became an official entity in 1945.

That's when all of the states that had ultimately adhered to the 1942 declaration and had declared war on Germany or Japan by March 1, 1945, were called to the founding conference held at San Francisco's Fairmont Hotel. Drafted in the hotel's Garden Room, the UN charter was signed on June 26 and ratified by the required number of states on October 24, which is now officially United Nations Day. The General Assembly first met in London on January 10, 1946.

Also at the summit, the 26 nations decided to locate the UN headquarters in the eastern United States. Ultimately, that location would become its present day home on the east side of Manhattan, because multimillionaire John D. Rockefeller, Jr., offered to buy a tract of land there to house the headquarters.

The United Nations' original charter reflected the will of mostly Western nations that were united against one common enemy during the war. Eventually, the effects of the Cold War and the changing of individual national leadership would make much of the original doctrine different today.

By the late 1950s, the expanded membership had begun to change the organization. In the early years, the nations were mainly in the West. As many Eastern nations began to join, voting patterns began to change. Soon the clear majority of the United States and its allies began to disappear.

For its part, of course, the Fairmont has become one of San Francisco's most famous hotels. It has become legendary for its fortitude in surviving its early years among the ruins of the Great San Francisco Earthquake in 1906. It has also hosted presidents from as far back as William Howard Taft, who visited shortly after the hotel opened to much fanfare. ●

1944

● **World Bank Established**
Preparing to rebuild the international economic system near the end of World War II, 730 delegates from the 44 Allied nations gathered at the Mount Washington Hotel in Bretton Woods, New Hampshire, for the United Nations Monetary and Financial Conference. The delegates deliberated upon, and signed, the Bretton Woods Agreements, which, among other things, established the World Bank.

1945

● **World War II Ends**
On August 15, 1945, Japan officially surrendered, bringing World War II to an end. In the aftermath, American GIs returned to the United States, and many of them had nowhere to go as their lives were changed forever. In the years following the war, hotels around the country were used to house veterans who were returning from both Europe and the Pacific.

1946

● **The King David Bombed**
On July 22, 1946, members of an underground movement, the Irgun, bombed the King David hotel in Jerusalem. The hotel housed the central offices of the British Mandatory authorities of Palestine. More than 90 Britons were killed in the attack.

Determined to develop a family-friendly lodging experience, Kemmons Wilson, with the help of children, cut the ribbon on his first Holiday Inn.

1950-1959

Life is a Highway

by Philip Hayward

In 1951, Kemmons Wilson, the 38-year-old future founder of the Holiday Inn hotel chain, decided to take his wife and children on vacation to Washington, D.C.

Though he was comfortably well off from his successful construction company, the Memphis, Tennessee, businessman nonetheless chose to drive his Oldsmobile the 800-plus miles to the nation's capital. After all, air travel was not the option it is now, as it was still new and very expensive, and railroads had apparently passed their prime. So, for a few dollars a night, the Wilson family could easily afford to bed down in any of the numerous motor hotels dotting the highways between the two cities. However, these "motels," as they had only recently come to be known, did not always offer the optimal travel experience. In fact, they frequently presented an array of unique problems, and Wilson was just the person to take note — and action.

For starters, Wilson quickly discovered that quality control in the hotel industry was nearly non-existent. At the time, the notion of quality was considered a manufacturing discipline, not a hospitality practice. Unsuspecting guests quickly learned that even the worst motels could look very nice from the outside. The only way to determine if the accommodations were adequate would be to personally step inside the lobby or guestroom. Simply stated, that practice alone aggravated the frugal-minded Wilson. Then there were the different room rates to consider. Single- and double-room occupancy costs were one thing, but motels were also charging for each child. As the Wilsons had five kids, this was not very cost-effective for family travelers. After experiencing a number of these properties firsthand, Wilson had vowed to get into the motel business and make positive changes. He believed that everyone in the country had an automobile, and sooner or later they would be driving somewhere in the United States ... and would need a clean, comfortable place to stay.

Wilson's wife, Dorothy, asked him, "How many are you going to build?" "Oh, about 450. That ought to cover the country," he replied. "And, if I never do anything else worth remembering in my life, children are going to stay free at motels."

His ambitious overhaul of the lodging industry, however, didn't happen overnight, but within a matter of years. His company, Holiday Inn, blew past the 450 property mark, and by the 1970s, the chain had three times as many rooms as his closest competitors, Sheraton and Ramada (208 and 939, respectively). Along the way, Wilson set the industry parameters for room size (12 feet by 30 feet), along with design, amenities, (including free TV), franchising, and development. Yet, for all he accomplished, little of it would have been possible a decade earlier, or even a decade later. In short, the forces at work in the1950s also enabled a multitude of changes that transformed the United States in that 10-year period — politically, culturally, and economically.

The Holiday Inn sign became a familiar sight to motorists during the 1950s.

● The **American Hotel Institute,** later to be renamed the **American Hotel & Lodging Educational Institute,** is launched.

● **Kemmons Wilson** opens his first **Holiday Inn** in Memphis, Tenn., named for the Bing Crosby movie.

● **The American Hotel Foundation** (now the American Hotel & Lodging Educational Foundation) is launched.

● **Howard Dearing Johnson** initiates the first **lodging franchise,** a motor lodge in Savannah, Georgia.

1950   1951   1952   1953   1954

In 1957, J. Willard Marriott opened the Twin Bridges Marriott Motor Hotel across the river from Washington, D.C.

Call it a confluence of events, but when the end of World War II ushered out the Great Depression, the U.S. economy exploded with a pent-up demand for goods and services that would help shape the U.S. lodging industry for years to come. Americans developed a yearning for the immediate — good, solid white-collar jobs with comfortable homes in the newly arisen suburbs. Fueled by the G.I. Bill, they received college diplomas and started working. They became serious consumers, purchasing TVs, refrigerators, air conditioning, and, most essential for the lodging industry, automobiles. By the time the 1950s rolled in, cars were cheaper, more reliable, and could cover greater distances. When the federal government undertook the massive, $77 billion Interstate Highway program, Americans began vacationing by car in even greater numbers.

With prosperity came a wave of new brands to join Holiday Inn — most notably Howard Johnson, Ramada, Red Lion, Marriott, and Vagabond Inns. In the highest tier, Laurence Rockefeller saw a niche in 1956 for a resort chain driven by superior levels of service and environmental stewardship that continues to this day. While it did not become a "brand" until 2009, construction of

the Fontainebleau Hotel in Miami Beach showed that hotels could be architecturally significant and hugely exciting at the same time. Well-to-do East Coasters gravitated to the hip Morris Lapidus-designed behemoth to "see and be seen" while enjoying Rat Pack entertainment.

In addition, the Global Hyatt Corporation we know today was born in 1957, with the acquisition of the Hyatt House at the Los Angeles Airport. Chicago businessman Jay Pritzker had heard that Hyatt von Dehn wanted to get out of the hotel business. Consequently, Pritzker bought his share in a $2.2 million deal, reportedly written on a napkin in the hotel's coffee shop.

For the American Hotel Association, the 1950s were no less tumultuous than what the country itself was experiencing. Although the association had its share of administrative and budgetary issues, it did not lack enthusiasm, drive, and self-aware-

> In the 1950s, many motels were built with swimming pools, which helped them compete with hotels.

- **J.W. Marriott** opens the **Twin Bridges Marriott Motor Hotel** in Arlington, Virginia.

- **Hilton** offers a **direct-dial** telephone service.

- **AHA** sells the license for the Universal TravelCard to **American Express.**

- **Sheraton** introduces **Reservatron,** the industry's first automated electronic reservation system.

1955   1956   1957   1958   1959

ness. In a 1950 poll of U.S. hoteliers, the well-respected E.M. Statler was chosen "Hotel Man of the Half Century." Characteristically, the designation was prestigious. It was announced in a grand banquet that was covered by national radio networks. The well-known broadcaster Edward R. Murrow even devoted five minutes of his show to profile Statler.

AHA (the "motel" moniker would not be applied for another couple of years) got its first taste of things to come when incoming President J.B. Herndon announced at his inaugural banquet his plans to authorize formation of an educational institution with Arthur Landstreet as its president. EI, as it came to be popularly known, was initially housed at Mississippi State University. Even though it was hard to argue with the merits of providing industry training for the hotel workforce, EI was not popular at first. AHA President Albert Pick even succeeded in raising $35,000 to support a non-AHA entity — seven times the operating budget of EI. It took the efforts of a small group of supporters to keep EI together before it hit its stride in the 1970s.

Aiming for business travelers, Western Hotels released a series of ads for its meetings facilities.

Arthur Landstreet, president of AHA's Educational Institute, had an interesting story for 'Tavern Talk' in a May 1955 issue.

AHA received its own refurbishing, beginning in 1952 during the presidency of Arthur J. Packard, who was practically a one-man association. Using his influence as president, chairman, *Hotel Red Book* president, chairman of the government affairs committee, and AHA finance chairman, Packard succeeded in bringing a more business-like approach and enhanced image to the association. He solidified that possibility with the hiring of Lawson A. Odde as AHA director of operations. A graduate of Yale University who studied hotel management, Odde most significantly revamped the AHA membership development program.

Interestingly enough, during this decade most AHA members viewed the rise of motels as a threat to their businesses and to the association. Apparently, motel owners tended not to normally join associations. "I am looking for managers who have never worked at a hotel or a motel, because I want people who haven't learned what you can't do," Kemmons Wilson is reported to have said. The rise of

Kemmons Wilson: Lodging for the Weary Traveler

by Cheryl Courtney Semick

For Charles Kemmons Wilson, it was personal. The creator of the Holiday Inn hotel chain lined America's new highways with welcome mats out of frustration from his own family vacation.

From Memphis to Washington, D.C., Wilson was increasingly annoyed by the random rules he encountered at the mom-and-pop motels along the way. Each stop solidified his resolve: he would build his own hotel chain.

While hoteliers pampered the rich, Wilson was happy to accommodate the rest, "the good Lord made more of them," he reasoned,

and so in 1952, the first Holiday Inn was built in Memphis, Tennessee, charging only $6 a night. By 1959, Holiday Inn had 100 properties that were providing standardized hotel services to America's open-road travelers.

Born in 1913 to an Osceola, Arkansas, insurance salesman who died when he was 9 years old, Wilson moved to Memphis with his mother, and out of financial necessity started his first business at age 7, assembling a sales force of 12.

Wilson wasn't one with small vision. With insatiable merriment, Wilson acquired land like a child "going on an Easter egg hunt," he said, "sometimes you find the golden egg." By the 1970s, Holiday Inn had reached across oceans.

TIME magazine reported in April, 1972, that Wilson, on average, opened "a new Holiday Inn every three days — or one new room every 36 minutes." He had 1,045 properties in 50 states and 20 foreign countries or territories, according to the article. The *TIME* cover boasted, "The Man With 300,000 Beds" and declared, "He has transformed the motel from the old way-

side fleabag into the most popular home away from home." In 1975 the chain peaked at 1,700 worldwide.

The magic of Wilson wasn't in the green, orange, and yellow signs that warmly welcomed wearied motorists the world over. It was far beyond clean linens and free nights for kids. The man behind the modern hospitality industry's global sensation had a simple plan: accommodate consistently. He was a "consummate entrepreneur," boasts his Web site, he "left an indelible stamp on the culture of American commerce." ●

Other Notables

● **John Willard Marriott**
Returning from a Mormon missionary trip to New England in 1921, Utah farm boy John Willard Marriott passed through Washington, D.C. Awed by the profitability of a street food-vendor, Marriott set his life course on service. In 1953, his restaurant chain went public; in 1957 he expanded to hotels.

● **Paul Grossinger and Jennie Grossinger**
Raised at the Grossinger's Catskills Resort Hotel, Paul Grossinger and his sister Elaine assumed the helm of their mother Jennie's hamlet in upstate New York at her death in 1972. Jennie Grossinger, a tour de force in hospitality, gained prominence in 1952 when her ski resort was the first to use artificial snow.

entire chains often caused independent owners and operators many sleepless nights, as newer players were cutting into their market share. Larger chains, franchisors, and referral companies came fully equipped with their own resources and convention-sized annual meetings. Still, the industry in the '50s was overwhelmingly independently owned and operated. It had decades to improve and innovate, which was necessary to keep pace and meet the needs of a rapidly evolving industry.

For years, Packard and New Orleans hotelier Seymour Weiss lobbied for AHA to develop its own credit card, a potentially lucrative venture. They succeeded by the mid-1950s — and the innovative Universal Travelcard was launched. Banks agreed to guarantee charges up to $500 and checks up to $250, provided AHA members would honor them. Despite its merits and vast potential, AHA members never warmed to the Travelcard. In a deal that would bring $2 million to the fledgling American Hotel Foundation, the card was transferred to American Express. Even today, American Express remain a supporter of AH&LA.

As the 1950s came to a close, AHA managed to reconcile the rivalry between EI and its own internal education department. EI, which by then had moved to the campus of Michigan State University in 1959, now oversaw the consolidated education services offered by the association.

Economically, the 1950s were turbulent, as supply grew twice as fast as demand. For the most part, the lodging industry's profitability would mirror the national economy. Its peak times of July 1953 and October 1956 were in close step with the general economy. Its tough periods — May 1950, December 1954, and November 1958, also matched the U.S. economic landscape. It was clear that when times were good people traveled more oftern.

Also, as more professionally trained, business-minded leaders rose through the ranks within the industry, hotels began to evolve architecturally. Many hotel lobbies began to shrink, but room size tended to increase — from an average of 150

A decade old, Best Western continued to shine in the 1950s, adding hotels in the western United States at a quick rate.

The Universal Travelcard was transferred to American Express for $2 million, which went to the Foundation.

Atlantic City's Boardwalk was a popular attraction in the 1950s, and large hotels rose along it.

Americans on the Move

by Dawn Marchadier

The 1950s are characterized as a decade of unprecedented economic and population growth for the United States. With increased prosperity came a higher demand for material goods as well as leisure activities. The automobile industry benefited significantly from this surge in spending; according to research, nearly 60 million cars were purchased during the 1950s. This newfound mobility led to increased travel for business — as well as fun and adventure.

Motels multiplied along the highways. But the face of these properties changed over the decade, just as highways started to appear across the nation. As described in the San Jose State University's History of the Motel: "Before long, small-time (family-run) motor courts were rendered obsolete by chains like Holiday Inn, that began to blur the distinction between motels and hotels. Single story structures gave way to double and triple-deckers. The thrill of discovering the unique look and feel of a roadside motel was replaced by assurances of (consistency) by hosts 'from coast to coast'."

Competition during this decade led to a quest for new guest-appealing ideas, and one of the most successful was the combination of the budget motel design with luxury concepts. Newly introduced larger rooms took the motel industry by storm. Even the smallest room amenities were not overlooked, as hotels now provided shower caps to protect guests' hairdos, as well as disposable cup dispensers equipped with metal cigarette holders.

In the 1950s, hotels made advancements in customer satisfaction techniques through the use of technology. The first outside glass elevator and first motorized moving sidewalk, the "Travolator," were installed at the El Cortez Hotel and Motel in San Diego, California. Year-round swimming was enabled at the Holiday Inn North of Memphis, Tennessee, through the use of a vinyl-coated, air-supported nylon pool dome. The Beau Rivage Motel in Bal Harbour, Florida, introduced a closed circuit television system that permitted "babysitting by video," allowing a child care professional to watch several children at one time from a panel of monitors in a control room. ●

1950
● The word **"motel"** entered dictionaries, a full 25 years after it was introduced on a sign along the Pacific Coast Highway.

1951
● **Hilton** became the first hotel company to install **television sets** in all guestrooms.

● Table-tent air-raid instructions and **"What to Do in Case of Enemy Attack"** cards appeared in hotel rooms.

1953
● The **Western Hills Hotel** in Fort Worth, Texas, offered its guests the **first heliport facility.**

1954
● The **American Hotel and Motel Association** created the first **travel credit card.**

1957
● **Marriott** opened the **Twin Bridges Motor Hotel** in Arlington, Virginia, with drive-through check-in.

1959
● **Master Video Systems** (MVS) introduced a revolutionary visual room control system, permitting room status information at a glance.

square feet to more than 300 square feet. Guestrooms and loobies began to become more elaborate as well.

In addition, food and beverage departments received makeovers. Prior to the '50s, food and beverage was considered a minor business concern. Instead, the emphasis tended to be placed primarily on quality. Hoteliers tried to break even while making sure never to lose much money in food and beverage. But in the 1950s, owners began demanding that food and beverage be promoted and operated along the lines of planning and procurement. For the first time, food and beverage was put on a for-profit basis. As Cornell University professor Gerald Lattin explained in an interview in *Lodging* magazine in the 1980s, chain operations drove this improvement.

Not surprisingly, the rise of motels began to shake apart old models of hotel profitability. With their simplicity of operation, low labor costs, and smaller sizes, they began to draw

attention to their bottom-line numbers. In 1951, *Business Week* magazine reported that motel owners were able to keep 34 cents out of each dollar earned as clear profit. At the time, the average motel consisted of 17 units, had an average daily rate of $4.46, and occupancies averaging 76 percent. In the early 1950s, motels were often small operations — "mom and pop" in nature, a status that quickly gave way as large chains formed and expanded. One example of these chains is Travelodge, which in the 1950s had 41 properties and was poised for dramatic growth.

Even larger-scale chains were getting in on the act. Marriott and Sheraton both brought their hotels to the exploding highway system in search of new customers. Marriott even had opened a sizeable roadside property with 356 rooms. In 1957, J. Williard Marriott opened his Twin Bridges Marriott, a motor hotel at the foot of the 14th Street Bridge on the Virginia side of the Potomac River, just across from Washington, D.C. Guests were able to conveniently drive to the edge of the nation's captial and still enjoy its landmark sites from afar.

During the decade of the 1950s, hotel guests were finding it almost impossible to tell the difference between hotels and motels, given such similarities as elevators, restaurants, pools, and other amenities. It was one reason AHA added "motels" to its name at the time. As one AH&MA member quipped: "If they hand me a key to a room and let me carry my bags, it's a motel; if they hand them to a bellboy, it's a hotel." **100th**

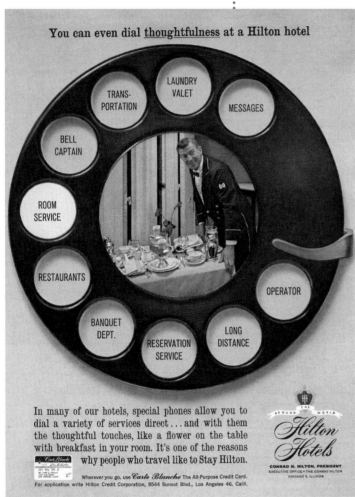

You can even dial <u>thoughtfulness</u> at a Hilton hotel

In many of our hotels, special phones allow you to dial a variety of services direct...and with them the thoughtful touches, like a flower on the table with breakfast in your room. It's one of the reasons why people who travel like to Stay Hilton.

Hilton Hotels

CONRAD N. HILTON, PRESIDENT
EXECUTIVE OFFICE • THE CONRAD HILTON
CHICAGO 5, ILLINOIS

Wherever you go, use *Carte Blanche* The All-Purpose Credit Card.
For application write Hilton Credit Corporation, 8544 Sunset Blvd., Los Angeles 46, Calif.

To capitalize on its one-of-a-kind direct dial telephones Hilton Hotels created a series of ads touting its service.

More Than Meets the Eye

by Matt Brinn

For $25, tourists in the tiny town of White Sulphur Springs, West Virginia, can visit an astounding relic of the cold war. The Greenbrier Bunker was a massive underground shelter constructed during the Eisenhower administration to house members of the legislative branch in the event of a nuclear apocalypse.

It was a high-security national secret for more than 30 years. Trusted with maintaining the facility and keeping it under wraps was the long-time staff of the luxurious Greenbrier hotel.

When Truman Wright, who ran the Greenbrier hotel from 1951 to 1974, was interviewed by *The Washington Post* in 1992, he was hesitant to talk about the secret bomb shelter. "I did not know for certain of anything that was going into it," he told Ted Gup, who published a revealing article on the subject. Wright was one of many hotel staff workers who were able to keep the bunker a secret when questioned by the press.

In addition to Wright, Gup interviewed the then current managing director of Greenbrier, Ted Kleisner. After touring through the Virginia Wing, an ornate ballroom, which also served as a secret entrance to the facility, Gup grilled Kleisner with a series of questions about the bunker. "How could that possibly go on without my total involvement?" he responded, "...our only role here is to serve guests."

In reality, a 112,544-square-foot living space was hidden behind two 20-ton blast doors underneath the Virginia Wing. When it was operational, the bunker could sustain more than 1,100 people. In the event of a nuclear holocaust, the shelter would serve as a base of operations for surviving members of Congress.

Wright, Kleisner, and a host of other workers at the Greenbrier Hotel were trusted with knowing the whereabouts of the government's most comprehensive contingency plan against a nuclear attack. Buried 25 feet under a five-star luxury resort was the facility that could save the United States government from absolute destruction. Thanks to the constant vigilance of a few incredible hoteliers, the Greenbrier Hotel successfully kept its secret. ●

1955

● **The Disneyland Hotel Saves the 'Magic Kingdom'**
Disneyland's opening day was plagued with mishaps. After some negative press, Walt Disney invited reporters to a series of private parties hosted at the luxurious Disneyland Hotel. Soon after, the park's profits soared.

● **The Plaza is Immortalized in Children's Fiction**
New York's prestigious Plaza Hotel gained considerable publicity when author Kay Thompson published Eloise, a fictional book detailing the troublesome exploits of a little girl who lives in the hotel.

1959

● **Las Vegas Convention Center Lures Gamblers**
A massive convention center was built in Las Vegas to fill hotel rooms with guests during the off-season. It included a 90,000-square-foot exhibit hall attached to a silver-domed rotunda that seated 6,300 visitors.

● **The Doors to Communist Cuba Close**
Prior to the communist revolution, Havana was a mafia-run tourist haven, boasting a plethora of hotels, nightclubs, and casinos. When Fidel Castro took power, the 'Latin Las Vegas' all but disappeared.

AMERICAN HOTEL & LODGING
EDUCATIONAL INSTITUTE

by Robert Steele

The American Hotel & Lodging Educational Institute (EI) has been serving the training and professional development needs of hospitality industry professionals for more than 55 years. Arthur Landstreet, a Tennessee hotelier and chair of AH&MA's Education Committee, first proposed an independent training organization to prepare hospitality personnel to fill the industry's many open management positions in 1949.

Industry response was lukewarm, but Landstreet managed to interest notable hotelier Conrad Hilton in his idea. J.B. Herndon, one of Hilton's vice presidents, embraced education as the focus of his AH&MA presidential platform, announcing the formation of the American Hotel Institute when he accepted the presidency in 1951.

EI had its birth at Mississippi State University in 1953, where the school's faculty worked closely with hospitality leaders throughout the country to determine the industry's training needs and to develop a 12-course home-study curriculum for middle managers. EI moved its offices to Michigan State University in the mid-1950s and consolidated with AH&MA's education department in 1959.

EI did not experience much growth or success in its first 25 years. But that would begin to change when E. Ray Swan joined the company as its executive director in 1978. He pledged that he would turn EI around in four months — or else he would resign. He kept his promise to turn EI around and therefore never faced the possiblity of following through on his resignation. Under Swan, EI introduced a number of new initiatives to help spur its success, including offering professional certifications, various courses, group study programs, management institutes, and executive academies. It also developed its first videotaped training resource.

Arthur Landstreet

Robert T. Foley was appointed president of EI in 1996. In 1997, he moved the company's headquarters to Orlando, Florida, while keeping the academic, allied divisions, and fulfillment center in Lansing, Michigan. In 1998, Anthony G. Marshall succeeded Foley as president.

In 2001, the organization's name was changed to the American Hotel & Lodging Educational Institute, reflecting the name change of its parent organization, the American Hotel & Lodging Association. It still kept the brand name of "EI." After Marshall's retirement in 2005, Scott Pierce was appointed president, followed by Roy Kennington, and I have served as EI's president since November 2008.

While EI's first students were working hospitality professionals, the scope of its educational reach expanded to include colleges and universities, many of which also use EI's hospitality textbooks and courses. Professors at university-level hospitality programs use individual EI textbooks, or adopt its turnkey curricula. Students also have the opportunity to earn EI's academic course certification in addition to the credentials offered by their college. In 1991, EI reached out to the high school career education market with the Lodging Operations Program (LOP), replaced in 1999 by the Lodging Management Program. By 2008, more than 600 high schools in 46 states offered this curriculum. In addition, since 2004, EI has hosted the LMP National Competition, which brings together teams of students to compete for scholarship money and national recognition.

Since 1971, more than 55,000 individuals have earned professional certification through EI. The Certified Hotel Administrator program was introduced in 1971, followed by front office and food and beverage certifications. In 1984, the Master Hotel Supplier program was developed to recognize industry suppliers; additional certifications for every level are now readily available.

In 1989, EI formalized its international licensing concept with the first Hospitality Educational Program (HEP) agreement. HEP licensees hold exclusive rights within a geographic territory to offer EI courses, to market and distribute EI products, and to train and certify faculty members and hospitality employees. EI also offers a Global Academic Program (GAP) license, through which international schools may offer EI courses and its curricula. Since the mid-1990s, EI has maintained an office in India.

Over the years, EI has also entered into several partnerhships with other organizations to help better promote imporatant issues to the general public and the lodging industry. In the early 1990s, EI worked with the National Easter Seals Society to produce videos to help properties comply with the Americans with Disabilities Act. In the mid-1990s, EI worked with the Club Managers Association of America (CMAA) to provide material for its professional certification program, as well as to develop other print materials. Other collaborations over the years have included those with several hospitality associations and training partners.

Throughout its history, EI has responded to industry needs with new programs and delivery methods that keep pace with the times. The first EI training video was produced in 1985. In 1996, EI introduced language-free videos for line-level training, responding to the needs of the hospitality industry's diverse workforce.

Meanwhile, EI has been quick to adapt to changing technology and preferences of information delivery. In 1999, EI began offering online, Web-based training, called Course-Line® and CyberCinema®. The online shopping cart for purchasing EI textbooks was launched in 2003, enabling customers to easily and securely order training materials order via the Internet. Today's online learning opportunities include the Professional Development Program, a series of 25 online modules in the areas of leadership, human resources, and technology; Supervisory Skill Builders Online, CARE® Online, and a CHA assessment tool.

EI is one of AH&LA's two not-for-profit affiliates, along with the American Hotel & Lodging Educational Foundation (AH&LEF). In May 2002, EI's board merged with the board of AH&LEF to provide greater operating efficiency and clarity between the affiliates. Both entities continue to operate as separate divisions. Both are also recipients of the generous portion of revenues generated by the Americas Lodging Investment Summit. AH&LEF was named a beneficiary of the summit, and the benefit it receives is divided between the AH&LEF and EI. ●

AMERICAN HOTEL & LODGING
EDUCATIONAL FOUNDATION

by Joori Jeon, CPA, CAE

The American Hotel & Lodging Educational Foundation (AH&LEF) was organized in 1953 for the purpose of holding American Hotel Credit Corporation stock (AHCC), which was established to create and operate the Universal Travelcard (UTC), one of the first credit cards generally accepted and used by the hotel industry. AH&MA, as a trade association, could not participate as a stockholder of a business corporation, and this arrangement provided any dividends paid to the Foundation would be used for educational purposes.

The original trustees were Arthur J. Packard of Packard Hotel Company; Carling Dinkler, Sr. of Dinkler Hotels; George Podd of Horwath & Horwath; Thomas Powell, and E. Leslie Sefton of Hotel Commodore.

No dividends were ever paid by AHCC, although it was successful enough to repay loans made by various hotel companies to provide original working capital. In 1956, the Foundation acquired all AHCC stock with a loan from AH&MA and became the sole stockholder. This loan was repaid in 1958, after the sale of UTC to American Express, which became necessary because AHCC did not have the finances to provide central billing. The Foundation received proceeds on renewals of the original UTC holders for more than 30 years.

Nearly half-a-million dollars were disbursed as educational grants and scholarships over the next 16 years without ever soliciting funds from the industry. It wasn't until the death of Arthur Packard in 1974 that active fundraising was engaged to build an endowment scholarship in his name (which is still considered the Foundation's most prestigious scholarship award). That same year, the Foundation's first employee was hired. Lawson Odde was named business manager and continued in this capacity for 10 years, after which he served as a scholarship consultant until his death in 1988.

Arthur Packard

Under the leadership of Foundation President Paul Handlery of Handlery Hotels, a study was commissioned in 1982 to poll industry representatives regarding the Foundation's future funding and programs. Based upon the results, the first major fundraising initiative, The Spirit of Achievement Campaign, was launched in 1983 to provide long-term support for the Foundation's general scholarship and education programs. The campaign attracted more than 100 donors contributing $3.9 million.

A few years later, Bob Stein of Gardner, Stein, and Frank, recognized an opportunity to raise money for the Foundation by providing a forum for hotel executives and lodging suppliers to network and engage in a little friendly competition. In 1988, he chaired the first annual Golf Classic at the Grenlefe Golf & Tennis Resort in Florida. It was a resounding success and remains a favorite today. A second special event was added to the Foundation's repertoire in 1993 when its first auction was organized. Today, the Big Apple Auction has evolved into an annual event at the International Hotel/Motel & Restaurant Show with more than 200 items being auctioned off.

Ten years after the conclusion of the Spirit campaign the Foundation's board, chaired by Allen Ostroff of Hotel Dynamics, Inc. (then with Prudential Realty Corp.), acknowledged that funds were required for a newly created research grant program as well as expansion of the scholarship programs. The Hospitality 2000: Building Leadership for the Future Campaign, chaired by Conrad Hilton, was launched with a goal of $6 million. By its conclusion, it had exceeded all expectations, raising $6.7 million from only 135 donors.

Following the capital campaign, many individuals and companies wanted to support the Foundation's programs, but couldn't do so on a large scale with a capital gift. The Annual Giving Drive was created to solicit smaller unrestricted gifts on an annual basis. The newest fundraising event is the Dinner Tribute, where AH&LA bestows its most prestigious honor, the Hospitality Heritage Award, upon an individual, family, or company in recognition of their leadership and commitment to the growth and prosperity of the industry.

In 2000, the Foundation's board, chaired by Thomas Hewitt of Interstate Hotels Corporation, took on its greatest challenge. Faced with a need to help the industry secure a trained workforce and to harness the efficient use of technology, the New Century Fund Campaign was launched. Chaired by Bill Marriott, the campaign yielded more than $9.3 million.

Since its inception, the Foundation has disbursed more than $14 million through its scholarship, educational, research, and workforce development programs. Scholarships still remain the Foundation's primary focus and account for almost half of its annual budget, with 10 academic scholarships programs being administered for undergraduate and graduate-level hospitality majors. Additionally, professional development scholarships are offered to hotel employees wishing to take distance learning or professional certification through EI, as well as scholarships for partner state association staff to attend the Institutes for Organizational Management.

Since 1995, more than $2.4 million has been granted through the Foundation's research program to address critical issues such as ADA requirements and technology advancement. Some of its most popular programs are: The Key to Best Practices in the U.S. Lodging Industry, a landmark study which describes 144 best practices at both the corporate and property levels; the Impact of Room Tax Increases documents the full impact of tax changes on sales, jobs, and government revenue; AH&LA's biennial Lodging Survey, provides a snapshot industry trends; and the Hotel Technology 101 Primer Series, offers easy-to-read manuals in 11 different technology-related areas.

In recent years, $1.3 million has been expended through workforce development and school-to-career programs, which encourage interest in lodging. Approximately 7,000 high school students have been enrolled in the Lodging Management Program, and Skills, Task, and Results Training is now in 121 workforce training locations in 34 states.

The Foundation's initial vision has expanded and taken on a much stronger mandate: ensuring a viable future for the entire lodging industry. In the years to come, it will continue to address critical areas to ensure the prosperity of the industry. ●

Seattle's monorail, built in 1962 for the World's Fair, picks up passengers near the Washington Plaza Hotel.

1960-1969

'Talking 'bout a Revolution'

by Leda Kopach

Paul Kantner of Jefferson Airplane has been quoted as saying, "If you can remember anything about the sixties, then you weren't really there." But there is so much worth remembering. The rampant drug use, hippies, and the 'Summer of Love' may characterize this era best from a popular culture perspective; however, the counter culture prevalent during this era is but one aspect of a colorful and turbulent decade. While the country was altered in many wasys during this time, so too was the hotel industry. Several social and technological advancements offered oppertunities for hoteliers to expand their businesses. Both also allowed them to offer new amenities to guests that would forever change the expectations of the American traveler.

After the nation rallied around the progressive ideals of the youngest president to ever hold office, Americans experienced a stunning blow with the assassination of the 35th U.S. President, John F. Kennedy, in 1963, followed by the murder of civil rights leader Dr. Martin Luther King, Jr., five years later on a balcony of the Lorraine Motel in Memphis. Two months later, yet another Kennedy tragedy shook the nation again with the assassination of presidential hopeful Robert F. Kennedy, who ran for office on the same progressive government principles as his brother. These tragic events and their aftermath greatly defined the social awareness and volatility that punctuated the 1960s. The passing of the Civil Rights Act of 1964 and the Voting Rights Act of 1965, as well as the escalation of America's involvement in the unpopular Vietnam War, all contributed to the revolutionary mood of the decade, while several technological advancements spearheaded the country's modernization that was unfolding.

In the '60s, there were some 23,000 hotels, 40,000 motels, and 170 hotel chains operating in the United States. Because of the many changes during this historic period, it only stands to reason that the hotel industry was similarly affected by the innovations of this decade. Beginning in the previous decade, the 1956 passage of the Interstate Highway System bill signed by then-President Dwight D. Eisenhower, enabled roadside hotels to be built off main arteries throughout the United States. The suburban sprawl had begun, and the highways allowed for greater travel opportunities as roadways were improved and more easily navigated.

With the proliferation of motels, AHA saw fit to change its name to better reflect the state of lodging in the United States. In 1963, the association ceased being called the American Hotel Association, and took on the moniker, the American Hotel & Motel Association (AH&MA).

Meanwhile, hotel brands such as Best Western, Sheraton, Choice Hotels (then Quality Courts United),

A Quality Courts motel in the 1960s. Quality Courts United would become Choice Hotels International.

● **Best Western begins using the crown logo** with a rope border to identify member properties.

● AHA changes its name to the **American Hotel & Motel Association (AH&MA)**.

1960	1961	1962	1963	1964

Hilton, and Holiday Inn proliferated around the country and continued in both their expansion and in their franchising efforts that began in the 1940s, growing into areas made more accessible by the highway system.

Early partnerships among some brands allowed for easier expansion efforts, but were later abandoned as companies smelled opportunity and forged ahead on their own. For example, from 1946 to 1964, Quality Courts United shared a marketing relationship with Best Western, whose properties were mostly located west of the Mississippi River and thus not in direct competition with Quality Courts United. While their relationship initially made sense, it didn't go well in the long run and the companies decided to end it in 1964. At that same time, Best Western expanded to the eastern United States, first being called Best Eastern and then later changed its name back to Best Western for better national brand recognition.

In 1960, transatlantic air travel also significantly improved with the development of the Boeing 707, a new airliner that could travel in half the time as its predecessors. it also contained improved amenities and accommodations.

The first in-flight movie was shown in 1968, making long flights more bearable. Cross-country flights also picked up speed, reducing trips to five hours from coast-to-coast. With improved accessibility, resorts and high-rise hotels sprung up in vacation destinations such as Los Angeles and Las Vegas since they could attract and welcome guests from anywhere in the country. Even previously remote regions such as Hawaii and Colorado's Rocky Mountains were accessible if you had the money to travel since flights were still considered very expensive and out of reach for most Americans.

While many of the hotel companies had already started opening properties internationally in the 1950s, the trend picked up steam as opportunities for consumer travel overseas became more affordable and prevalent in this decade. Intercontinental Hotels, started by parent company Pan American Airlines as a means of providing passengers' lodging accommo-

Outdoor swimming pools, such as this one at the Holiday Inn in Concord, California, made a splash in the 1960s.

Best Western called its eastern U.S. operations Best Eastern, but returned to its original brand moniker.

Best Western becomes the first hotel company **to be wholly governed by a board of directors** made up entirely of its own member hoteliers.

Westin establishes **24-hour room service.**

The Atlanta Regency (now Hyatt Atlanta Regency) opens. It features a 21-story atrium.

Chain hotels such as Travelodge, Holiday Inn, and Howard Johnson's **begin to offer swimming pools** as a means of increasing revenue.

1965   1966   1967   1968   1969

dations along on its routes developed 11 hotels in Latin America, the first in the industry for that area of the world, during the 1950s as well as in Paris and London. In 1960, the hotel group added more properties in Vienna and Frankfurt, before building three more in Ireland the next year. Intercontinental also debuted the Six Continents Club, which was the lodging industry's first global guest-recognition program. More companies would soon go international, opening hotels quickly.

Members of AH&MA's Resort Committee pose for a photo in 1961.

Around since 1919, Hilton Hotels celebrated several milestones and infamous events during this decade. In 1960, Conrad Hilton passed the reins of the company he founded to his son, Barron, but remained chairman of the board of Hilton Hotels Corporation. Four years later, Hilton International spun off as a separate corporation as the company's presence grew overseas.

Other than the famous Bed-In for Peace event held by John Lennon and Yoko Ono in 1969 at the Amsterdam Hilton, one of the other most remembered events of 1968 also occurred at a Hilton property, specifically the Conrad Hilton in Chicago, during the Democratic Convention. Severe rioting across the street from the hotel in Grant Park caused management at the hotel to lock its doors for the first time ever for fear of violence.

Meanwhile, Sheraton had already made its foray into the international arena by this time, but its presence grew by leaps and bounds during this decade. By 1965, Sheraton had opened its 100th property.

Welcoming and attracting more tourists to visit the United States was all part of President Kennedy's New Frontier agenda, and during his watch, Congress established the U.S. Travel Service in the Department of Commerce with the intent of increasing the numbers of international visitors to the United States. As attracting more visitors only stood to benefit the lodging industry, AH&MA proceeded to give the government effort its help in promoting international travel.

And tourists weren't the only ones traveling to America. Entrepreneurs from countries such as India were looking for their American dream as they immigrated to the United States, many in search of sound investment opportunities, such as economy-scale hotels. Beginning in the '60s and continuing into the next decade, U.S. immigration laws were soft, granting residency rights for new arrivals investing more than $10,000 in a new business. Turns out, that was all that was necessary to buy into an economy-scale hotel at the time. For many immigrants, the opportunity was too good to pass up, and they created family businesses that have survived generations and continue to be a force in the industry.

Laurance Spelman Rockefeller:
Luxury in Paradise

by Cheryl Courtney Semick

Among the numerous ventures of Laurance Spelman Rockefeller is his savvy assimilation of luxury hotel resort structures and amenities into tropical landscapes.

In 1952, Rockefeller was sailing in the Caribbean when he envisioned his Caneel Bay resort on Saint John in the U.S. Virgin Islands. He worked to develop an infrastructure of roads, power, and fresh water on the small island before building the actual resort.

The Dorado Beach resort also received his special attention to detail. He would not allow any roof to be higher than the nearest palm tree. Hence, the guestrooms are two-story structures that face the Atlantic Ocean.

As a conservationist, Rockefeller believed that nature can be enjoyed in a resort setting without disturbing its natural ambience. His vision to create exclusive sanctuaries on such quiet Caribbean beaches as Caneel Bay and Dorado Beach in the mid-1950s gained him a reputation as a top hotelier and soon drew the attention of Hawaii Governor William F. Quinn.

It was 1960 when Rockefeller received an invitation from Quinn to develop a beachside resort on the Big Island's western shore. Circling the island by air, Rockefeller asked the Governor if he could go for a swim at Kauna'oa Beach. Inspiration came in the crystal waters as he stared back at the world's highest island mountain peak, Mauna Kea.

By the early '60s, Rockefeller's collection of hotel properties were known as RockResorts Inc., containing nine vacation sites with Mauna Kea Beach Hotel being the most expensive hotel ever built at that time for $15 million. Opening in 1965 with 154 guestrooms at the "exorbitant" nightly rate of $43 per night, including breakfast and dinner, the Mauna Kea quickly received honors. *Esquire* named it one of the "three greatest hotels in the world," and *Fortune* magazine named it one of the "10 best buildings of 1966." The Mauna Kea was also presented with an honors award by the American Institute of Architects.

Rockefeller had a knack for capturing the colors and flavors of natural landscapes. His strong belief that buildings should not intrude on the natural surroundings ushered in what is now known as "ecotourism." ●

Other Notables

● **Paul Handlery**
Paul Handlery built his first hotel, Handlery Motor Inn, in 1964. The property was connected to his father's Hotel Stewart in San Francisco. Harry and Paul owned the 'largest family run hotel chain in the world' by the mid-1950s with 26 properties, but are best known for creating the first pool bar featuring underwater ballet in their Stardust Hotel.

● **Curtis L. Carlson**
Turning his 1962 purchase of the Radisson Hotel in Minneapolis into an international brand, Curtis L. Carlson earned the remarkable title of 'ultra-entrepreneur' worldwide. He catapulted Carlson Companies Inc. to the pinnacle of the global market.

Motel 6 got its name from the $6 price of a room at its original property.

Motel 6 was established in 1962 in Santa Barbara, California, the first budget hotel at the time. Owners William Becker and Paul Greene decided on a $6 per night room rate based on expenses, thus the name, Motel 6. Recently, the chain, now owned by Accor Hotels, opened its 1,000th hotel in Biloxi, Mississippi.

Technological innovations at this time, especially in terms of computer development and usage, started making an impact in the lodging industry. Among those innovations was the first computerized central reservation system, which was established in 1964. And, as travel options increased and more and more Americans turned to the road to travel, the

Opened in 1962, the first Motel 6 in Santa Barbara, Caifornia, helped introduce the budget motel sector to the United States.

competition among hotel groups began to increase, spawning improvements in an array of both customer service and guest amenities, many of them based on the new technologies emerging at the time.

Since President Kennedy served only half of his term, from 1961-1963, he had barely dented his ambitious agenda. This included, among other broad issues, cracking down on questionable business expenses, which could have affected the profitability of lodging establishments. In 1961, Kennedy sent a proposal to Congress placing a per diem ceiling for all business expense accounts for income tax purposes and banning all entertainment expenditures. This legislation could have halted many planned business meetings at lodging establishments across the country, but AH&MA intervened on its members' behalf. By the time the law was passed in 1962, the legislation established that as long as the expense was a bona fide business expense, the expense was deductible.

As Lyndon B. Johnson stepped into the presidency in 1963 and introduced his own plan, calling it the New Frontier, he petitioned strongly for the passage of civil rights legislation, extensive coverage of federal wage and hour laws, and expansion of the area redevelopment program, among other issues. Two of the biggest issues for the hotel industry were, of course, the federal wage and hour law, a constant battle for AH&MA during this time, and the fight to keep tips classified as self-employment income for the employee. In the closing days of the 88th Congress in 1964, AH&MA successfully helped defeat a bill that would have imposed a tax on tips for Social Security purposes. In the spring of 1965, President Johnson recommended covering hotels, motels, and restaurants under the fed-

Competition Stimulates Advancement

by Gene G. Fiducia

The 1960s is often considered one the most significant decades in the history of hospitality, as this time period is marked by a variety of major changes and innovations that directly impacted the way people travel. Much of this progress was inspired by industrywide competition that affected all hotels — from upscale properties to privately owned budget motels.

Beginning with the development of the United States interstate highway

system in 1957, and culminating in 1965 with the Highway Beautification Act, travelers during this time were afforded easier access to most destinations across the country. Augmented by the convenience and ease of airplane travel, the 1960s saw many more travelers — across the social and economic spectrum — on the road and in the air. The ensuing influx of hotel guests resulted in increased development of properties along highways and near airports. In addition, during this decade more than 70 million children of the baby boom became teenagers and young adults, many of whom were searching for new experiences — and ready to explore America and beyond.

Although this surge of travelers brought good fortune to many hotel and motel owners, some "off the road" establishments often experienced a downturn in occupancy during this decade. Those hotels without a prime, high-traffic location experienced serious competition as the growing number of franchised properties that appeared in the 1950s, continued to expand into the 1960s. However, some independent owners turned to referral organizations that provided smaller hotels and motels with nearly the same advertising power that benefitted the franchises, thus gaining back a portion of the market share. ●

1960

● **Refrigerated minibars** were introduced by German company **Siegas.**

● The **Jack Tar Hotel** in San Francisco introduced an **automatic check-in system** with a TV monitor to greet guests, and room key delivery by pneumatic tube.

1962

● **Matthew Bernatsky**, professor at Cornell University, recommended that hotels add **bomb shelters** to the list of guest protections.

1964

● **Wheelchair accessible** guestrooms were introduced by the hotel chain, **Travelodge**.

1965

● The 240-room **Flagship Hotel** in Galveston, Texas, was **built on a pier** that extended 1,500 feet into the Gulf of Mexico.

1968

● The first **in-room minibar** was introduced at the **Madison Hotel** in Washington, D.C.

1969

● **New uniforms** reflected a changed look for **Marriott** employees.

eral wage and hour law to the 89th Congress, with double time for overtime and wider coverage and extended benefits under the unemployment insurance system.

During the House subcommittee hearing, four AH&MA witnesses testified, opposing coverage of the industry, and the association continued to offer experts opposing the legislation. While it looked like it was to pass in the House of Representatives, the House adjourned, postponing any action until 1966. Afterwards many concessions were made through each legislative step, so when the lodging industry was covered, only some hotels and motels were included, and they came in at a lower minimum wage, without penalty for overtime hours worked and with a number of credits that could be applied against the established wage. After 28 years of exemption, only some of the industry was partially covered when President Johnson signed the legislation on September 23, 1966.

As part of President Johnson's Great Society program, the Job Corps was created in 1964, giving at-risk and underprivileged youths academic and vocational training that would prepare them for the job market and end the cycle of poverty. Hotels also started to be converted for Job Corps use and for homes for the elderly.

While Washington, D.C., was buzzing with legislative issues, hotels in the south were in the middle of one of the country's biggest societal issues in history, as segregation was still a rampant problem in 1962. Following the desegregation of schools that took place in Atlanta, the National Association for the Advancement of Colored People (NAACP) decided to hold its convention in the city that year, hoping to pressure area hoteliers into desegregating hotels — but to no avail. While some hotels relaxed some of their segregationist policies at the time, most quickly reverted, closing the doors on African-Americans looking to patronize their establishments. There was a call for volunteer desegregation of hotels and restaurants for a couple years following, but most establishments, for fear of losing business, kept their doors closed to African-Americans, and even for interracial groups looking to share a meal. Finally, the Civil Rights Act was signed into law in 1965, empowering the federal government to oversee voter registration and elections, banning discriminatory literacy tests, and expanded voting rights for non-English speaking American citizens.

While many advancements were made, the 1960s were just the beginning, as social and racial equality were still fledgling notions in some parts of the country. 100th

U.S. hotel companies began rapidly expanding overseas in the 1960s. Intercontinental opened in Managua, Nicaragua.

The Times Turn Violent

by Len Vermillion

It's unfortunate that for all of the great accomplishments of the 1960s, the decade is marred by the tragic memories of three of history's most important assassinations, and two of them took place in hotels. The Ambassador Hotel (now demolished) in Los Angeles will forever be linked to the gruesome photos of Robert F. Kennedy sprawled lifelessly on the kitchen floor, a busboy grasping his hand, as the young presidential candidate lay dying from a bullet fired by Sirhan Sirhan. And, who will ever be able to suppress the horrible images of a slain Dr. Martin Luther King, Jr., on the balcony of room 306 at the Lorraine Motel (now the National Civil Rights Museum) in Memphis? His aides scurrying to tend to him, point toward where the shots by James Earl Ray were fired.

Combined with the assassination of President John F. Kennedy in Dallas, the premature deaths of these men touched off furors around the globe in the forms of rioting and conspiracy theories. They also helped lead to stalled federal legislation finally getting enacted.

In 1968, during the Democratic primary, Kennedy was in Los Angeles for the California vote and four hours after the polls closed, he claimed victory and addressed his supporters in the Ambassador's Embassy Room. When he finished speaking, his aides ushered him through the hotel's kitchen to quickly meet the press horde. As he was escorted, surrounded by a mob of aides and hotel staff, Kennedy shook hands with busboy Juan Romero. At that moment, Sirhan stepped down from a low tray-stacker and repeatedly fired a .22 caliber pistol. The nation watched the news coverage in horror.

Just months earlier, the assassination of Martin Luther King came as a shock to the country. On April 4, 1968, King, known as the face of the Civil Rights Movement, was gunned down as he stood on his balcony with aides. They had come to Memphis to support striking African-American sanitation workers. One day earlier, he had delivered his final speech, known as the "I've Been to the Mountaintop" address. The group was still in Memphis the next day due to a bomb threat against King's plane. ●

1960

Castro Checks into Hotel Theresa
Fidel Castro came to New York City to address the United Nations, and he stayed at what is affectionately called "The Waldorf of Harlem." His check-in causes a media circus and during his stay, Soviet Union Premier Nikita Khushchev paid him a visit, giving the hotel what the *New York Times* called "an enduring place in Cold War history."

1964

The Driskill Hosts LBJ
Lyndon B. Johnson always returned to the place he met his wife in 1934. The hotel served as his campaign headquarters through his congressional career. During the night of the 1964 presidential election, LBJ watched the returns and addressed supporters following his victory. During his term, the hotel became somewhat of a western base for the administration.

1968

Riots Disrupt the Democratic Convention
The turbulent times spilled over into the Democratic National Convention in Chicago, which became a battleground between police and protesters of the Vietnam War. Of the countless images and videos of the riots that ensued, the most enduring is a photo of police assaulting protesters outside of the Conrad Hilton hotel.

The Radisson in Minneapolis grew to become a center of the city's downtown throughout the '60s and '70s.

1970-1979

Destinations Unto Themselves

by George VonAllman

Two axioms define the state of the lodging industry in the decade of the 1970s. One comes from an ancient riddle: "What came first … the chicken or the egg?" The other comes from pop culture (specifically, the popular movie *Field of Dreams*): "If you build it, they will come!"

In 1970s, few hotels and resort destinations had enough function space and guestrooms to book convention groups. Instead, they relied on business travelers, as well as vacationing and transient guests. This was true for both independent and brand-affiliated properties. But that began to change as hotels started to build enough functional space to not only accommodate banquets and receptions, but also business meetings.

79

Today, of course, the group meeting and convention market is recognized as one of the most significant segments necessary to ensure room occupancy in hotels. Possibly the best example of this new dimension in driving occupancy levels for hoteliers was reflected in the growth that began in 1977 of one particular hotel located in a secondary, interior city and with no gambling/casino drawing power.

The Opryland Hotel originally featured 600 guestrooms, a 20,000-square-foot ballroom, and 30,000 square feet of convention space. Six years after opening, the property completed its first major expansion, dubbed "Phase II". This large undertaking added 467 guestrooms, moving the total to 1,067. Phase II also brought 30,000 square feet more of ballroom space, and added the hotel's first signature atrium, the Garden Conservatory.

Under large panes of glass filled with plant life and fountains, the Garden Conservatory was designed to allow guests to experience a walk in a tropical garden without going outdoors. Hundreds of rooms had balconies overlooking the conservatory, a truly unique feature that the hotel offered, and it set the stage for two more expansions of the hotel over the ensuing decades.

So where was all this incredible demand for meeting space and sleeping rooms coming from? A great part of the explanation was the evolution of Mutual Benefit Organizations (MBOs) in the United States. MBOs were non-profit organization established to provide benefits to its members (individuals or organizations) rather than to others or to the society as a whole. Usually referred to as associations and co-ops, these types of organizations almost doubled in numbers in the last quarter of the 20th Century. Between 1975 and 1995, their revenue grew by a whopping 155 percent.

Were developers and hoteliers of the '70s building hotels with the type of meeting space and complimentary public space (multiple food/beverage outlets and open, comfortable "pre-function" space) as a result of this

At a 'Serving the International Visitor' workshop held by AH&MA, attendees reviewed international symbols aimed at easing the language barrier.

● **Cecil B. Day** opens the first Days Inn on **Tybee Island, Georgia**.

● The Fabulous Flamingo changes its name to **the Flamingo Hilton Hotel**.

● Properties are required to **accept six major credit cards**. Hotel reservations that were charged were considered "guaranteed" and a hotel room had to be held for the entire night. Properties had the right to **bill for "no show" clients**.

1970　1971　1972　1973　1974

burgeoning new stream of group business? Or, was it more a function of the less feverishly growing traditional group business — all lumped in the same segment typically referred to as "corporate group"? And with construction loans and tax write-offs for hotels ramping up to their peak in the early 1980s, why not build "bigger" and "better" than what more conservative prognostication might dictate?

The 1970s were also years that saw further consolidation of hotel rooms. Many of the mom and pop roadside motels began to raise flags of major brands. Even more consolidation came about as the result of the rise of suburban mixed-use developments where retail/office space began to merge with hotel space. These "suburban hotels," as they were often referred to, were on everyone's drawing board, with the variations of size and architecture merely a function of the supporting business and residential economic strata.

On the lower-end, the traditional shopping mall with nearby light commercial and office space gave birth to Holiday Inn's Holidome to handle the requisite needs of travelers. On the higher-end, extensive renovation of aging dock/warehouse space was transformed into the signature Joseph

Art Linkletter served as a speaker, and posed for photos with attendees, at a 1977 AH&MA event in Seattle, Washington.

Rouse developments (such as Boston's Faneuil Hall, Baltimore's Harborplace, and Norfolk's Waterside, with a seamlessly attached branded hotel.

In addition to all the dramatic changes in the "bricks and mortar" arena, hotel staffing, especially in the sales and marketing area, was also growing and adapting to the changing marketplace. If you were an experienced hotel sales person who had expertise in corporate group and association markets, you were only one "cog" in the sales office of the 1970s. Also, a "unique" industry moniker had its origins in this timeframe because of the need for group "niche" segments. This term would have many outsiders believing

In 1972, AH&MA changed its logo to include the 'house' image present in today's logo.

● **Marriott** opens its 1st European hotel in **Amsterdam, Holland.**

● *Lodging* magazine is authorized as the official publication of AH&MA.

● **Best Western** begins its push for foreign expansion. Affiliation agreements are signed with 411 properties in **Australia** and **New Zealand.**

● **Hyatt** names its first woman general manager, **Cheryl Phelps,** to the former Queen Mary Hyatt in Long Beach, California.

1975　　　1976　　　1977　　　1978　　　1979

that many hotels were somehow busy chasing little blue cartoon characters, commonly known as "smurfs." In reality, the term SMURF was invented to cover a good portion of "Social-Military-Union-Religious-Fraternal" (respectively) groups. Along with this expansion and specialization in the

more than 1,000 individuals in the organization's membership base.

In the middle of the decade Best Western made the decision to drop its referral organization image, eliminating the word "motel" from its name. The move began its present day position as a direct competitor of other full-service hotel lodging chains.

The 1970s also saw the arrival of notable international hotel companies to the United States. In 1973, the first Sofitel hit U.S. shores, and in 1976, America's bicentennial celebration year, Four Seasons entered the United States with its first U.S. management contract in San Francisco for The Clift. After a facelift, *Condé Nast Traveler* named The Clift the number one hotel in America. It was also in the '70s that Four Seasons brought the concept of in-room amenities to the table in the luxury sector. In-room amenities quickly became popular across all levels of hotels, and in the mid-1970s, two Florida hotels ushered in the movie era when they began to offer HBO on their in-room televisions. Soon, "Free HBO" would become a popular sign outside of hotels, right next to the vacancy/no vacancy signage.

The Sahara Hotel's chief operator Mary Morris reviews handling incoming calls with a hotel operator at the main switchboard.

hotel's sales office, their counterparts (the meeting planners for the various MBOs) and SMURF groups were also on the rise and gaining in recognition and professional prestige within their organizations. Meeting Planners International (MPI) was started in Dayton, Ohio, in 1972 with 159 members. By the end of the decade, there were

It was also about the same time that Cecil B. Day, founder of the Days Inn franchise, began handing out wooden nickels to guests over the age of 50. It was the first "seniors programs" created in the industry.

The 1970s also saw the beginnings of the American Hotel & Motel Association's new publication, *Lodging*.

Jack DeBoer:
The All-Suite Concept

by Andrea Morabito

Jack DeBoer, best known to the hotel industry as the forefather of the extended-stay concept, didn't come up with the idea after careful thought and planning, but instead by chance. In the 1970s, he was a successful apartment developer whose company had built more than 16,000 apartments in 25 states. In fact, *National Real Estate Investor* magazine had named him the second-largest multi-family developer in the United States. Then interest rates rose to 20 percent, and the only way to finance new structures was to secure lodging rates — thus the residence-style hotel was born.

In 1975, DeBoer built the first Residence Inn in his hometown of Wichita, Kansas. The term "extended-stay" was first suggested by an intern at a Dallas advertising agency, and DeBoer liked it so much he adopted it to describe his new company.

The extended-stay concept resonated with business travelers, who stayed in town for more than seven days and were often underserved by current lodging options. The unique features include rates that drop the longer you stay, and weekly maid service instead of daily. The suite-style units are larger than traditional rooms and include a full kitchen. Complimentary breakfast and nightly social hours offer a feeling of community.

DeBoer built or franchised 103 Residence Inns before selling the company to Marriott Corporation. In the following decades, DeBoer founded second- and third-generation all-suite chains, Summerfield Hotel Corporation and Candlewood Hotel Company, respectively. He built both into successful brands: Summerfield grew to 25 hotels and is now owned by Hyatt Hotels Corporation, while Candlewood was bought by Intercontinental Hotels Group with 120 hotels. The extended-stay concept is now a mainstay. ●

Other Notables

● **Barron Hilton**
In 1971, Barron Hilton purchased the International Hotel and the Flamingo, bringing the credibility of the Hilton brand to the Las Vegas Strip. If the world's largest hotel chain could see the benefits of the gaming industry, so too could lending institutions. Without the Hilton stamp of approval, the ensuing building boom of the 1980s and 1990s may not have had such a large impact.

● **John Portman**
In 1967, architect John Portman built the Atlanta Regency as an impressive atrium hotel. Portman's radical project led him on a path as one of the premier hotel architects and developers of the 70s, and into the modern times. As he pioneered the role of architect as developer, he has said that he drew on a philosophy of self-reliance.

● **Steve Wynn**
In 1971 Steve Wynn purchased a one-acre slice of land next to Caesars Palace in Las Vegas, and then sold it to the resort for $2.25 million. He used the money from the land deal to buy a controlling interest in the Golden Nugget, where he elevated its status from a gambling hall to a resort hotel and casino, attracting a new upscale clientele. Today, he is the city's most recognized developer.

Under founding editors James A. and Frances Pearson, *Lodging* first published in 1975. Today, it has an industrywide circulation of more than 40,000 readers.

AH&MA's 1976 leaders get down to business setting priorities for the upcoming year.

Before establishing *Lodging* magazine, James and Frances Pearson were editors of the *Southern Hotel Journal*.

Some other innovations from the 1970s that would change hotels, both in terms of technical advances and improved services for guests, included the advent of toll-free phone numbers. For hotels, 1-800 numbers that directly connected guests to automated reservation systems opened an easier way of booking rooms. Many guests, in particular frequent business travelers, could simply call from anywhere in the United States to book a room or check availablity. This system would hold up as a primary force in reservation taking until the mid-1990s, when the Internet evolved from its military roots to a consumer presence. It wasn't long until online travel Web sites emerged.

James and Frances Pearson founded *Lodging*. The magazine was authorized as the offical publication of AH&MA in 1975.

Of course, franchising was growing in the 1970s, as Kemmons Wilson redefined the lodging business when his Holiday Inns began to pop up along interstate highways at every turn. However, the next logical step was the further segmentation of the major franchising brands, catering to the more clearly identified "strata" of individual and group guests. In the 1970s, the industry began to see the market sector definitons often used today.

Several popular brands that started to proliferate in the 1970s acquired the designation of "limited service" hotels (also known as "select service" hotels). But two of the first ones were arguably among

Implementing New Infrastructure

by Berenice Mendez

A dynamic progression of technological advancements spiked in the 1970s. Improvements were offered on all fronts from the guestroom to the reservation process. In the '70s, Quality Courts made hotel reservations possible any time of the day when it came out with an enhanced toll-free 24-hour reservations system. It also introduced new hotel billing centers to streamline the process of running its business.

Meanwhile, hotels in this decade became more entertaining than ever. In-room movies for guests were first offered in 1973 at the Sheraton-Anaheim.

Soon after, cable television was launched and in-room entertainment was further enhanced. In 1976, in-room HBO was first offered by two hotels in Florida, and a year later it, Showtime, and The Movie Channel became commonplace at hotels around the country.

Such innovations begat even more expectations when it came to guest services. At the time, many hotels undergoing construction or renovations added high-tech amenities and innovative designs. Meanwhile, hotel chains, such as Four Seasons, were busy setting a new standard in customer service. The luxury chain began providing amenities such as newspapers that were delivered along with breakfast, as well as overnight laundry service. Soon other hotels were getting more creative to help set their service and facilities apart from the crowd. In 1975, Hyatt differentiated itself by introducing the first "club" floor — the upscale Regency Club — to its guests.

The 1970's brought increased competition on all levels of the hospitality and travel industries, as lower airfares and attractive hotel rates provided more opportunities for people to travel to different parts of the world. Hotel guests' expectations were increasingly raised during this period, as they experienced several new types of luxuries and amenities at a variety of hotels across the United States. ●

1970

● **The Boeing 747** aircraft was introduced. It could haul more passengers at once and helped usher in less expensive airfares that in turned increased the number of travelers.

● Hotel companies such as **Hilton** and **Holiday Inn** expanded rapidly. At the time, a new Holiday Inn opened **every 2.5 days**, which led to the chain becoming the **first billion-dollar lodging company**.

1972

● **Quality Courts** (later known as Choice Hotels) switched to franchising without requiring strict rules or guidelines to follow.

● **Holiday Inn debuted its Holidome,** indoor swimming pools that effectively turned many of its properties in roadside resorts.

1973

● For the first time, **motel rooms** in the United States outnumber hotel rooms.

1974

● The first hotel "seniors program" was established **by Cecil B. Day and his Days Inn chain**. The program offered guests over 50 years old wooden nickels which could be collected and exchanged for discounted rooms.

AH&MA's Quality Environment Committee was started in 1979 with Al Kudrle in charge.

The 1970s were marred by a gas shortage. The lack of fuel kept travelers off the road.

the most significant: Budgetel arrived on the scene in 1978, and Choice Hotels bought Royal Inns, debuting Quality Royale, one of the precursors of the all-suite hotel. Quality Royale launched in 1979.

As the decade drew to an end, the stage was set for mass market segmentation. Soon customers would begin to identify different types of hotels by their service levels. Branding would often be associated with these mass market segmentation terms. The names of many hotel brands would become somewhat synonymous with their service lev-

els and their properties' offerings. During this time there was a huge series of changes undertaken in the assessment and building of brand loyalty.

The massive databases of customer information assembled by Marriott Hotels (among others) for its Marriott Rewards program had its beginnings with downloadable personal preferences gleaned from the "1-800" phone numbers and automated reservation systems pioneered in the 1970s. Today, those principles are at least partially responsible for a number of the guest satisfaction and customer service marketing programs that hotels use today.

After enduring political scandal and an unpopular war at the beginning of the decade, a gas shortage and inflation in the later years, and closing out with turmoil in the Middle East, the '70s gave way to the dawn of the '80s and a new chapter was about to unfold. With a changing political and economic landscape ahead, hoteliers prepared for the next challenges. **100**th

Politics, Scandal, and Rock 'n' Roll

by Shelley Seale

The upheaval of the 1960s seemed destined to continue into the 1970s. The civil rights and feminist movements were bucking the status quo, while the Vietnam War remained in the headlines. These issues and others created a growing disillusionment with the United States government, which came to a head with the Watergate scandal.

On June 17, 1972, five men were arrested inside the Democratic National Committee's office in the Watergate Hotel, and charged with attempted burglary and attempted telephone wire-tapping. The resulting investigation revealed an immense scope of crime and conspiracy including political espionage, campaign fraud, and illegal slush funds. All those involved were convicted, and all were employed by President Richard Nixon's re-election committee. Nixon and his staff conspired to cover up the break-in, but ultimately the president faced impeachment and resigned his presidency on August 9, 1974.

During this decade, celebrities such as musicians and movie stars began using their fame to promote political causes more than ever before. The seemingly separate worlds of entertainment and politics began to meld as anti-war songs topped the charts, and movies such as *The Candidate* and *All The President's Men* focused on political corruption. Activists such as John Lennon often found themselves the target of FBI surveillance.

Not all musicians were distracting themselves from the excesses of fame, however. The legendary "Riot House" – the Hyatt Continental Hotel on Sunset Boulevard in Los Angeles – was home to many touring rock bands and their accompanying parties, which earned the hotel its nickname. The famous Whiskey a Go Go club was located at the hotel, which was known for the wild antics of bands such as Led Zeppelin and The Who. Members of The Rolling Stones once threw televisions from the balconies. Even today, the newly renamed and remodeled Andaz West Hollywood doesn't hide its rock 'n' roll heritage under a blanket of respectability – instead, it flaunts it. ●

1970
● **Joplin Overdoses at the Landmark**
Janis Joplin passed away as the result of a heroin overdose at the Landmark Motor Hotel in Hollywood, California.

1974
● **Marriott Books Danno**
The Ilika Hotel in Honolulu, which was made famous by the opening sequence of the smash television hit Hawaii Five-O, was sold to Marriott.

1977
● **The International Creates a Furor**
The International Hotel in San Francisco evicted hundreds of low-income residents, primarily elderly Filipino and Chinese, sparking a protest of thousands and a focus on low-cost housing.

1978
● **Sid & Nancy at the Chelsea**
Nancy Spungen is stabbed to death by her boyfriend, Sid Vicious of the rock band the Sex Pistols, at the Chelsea Hotel in New York City.

● **The Filming of 'California Suite'**
Neil Simon's hit play 'California Suite' was turned into a hit movie. With stars Alan Alda and Jane Fonda on the set at the Beverly Hills Hotel, the legendary movie was made and went on to receive a Oscar nomination for Best Adapted Screenplay.

In 1981, Kimpton Hotels & Restaurants debuted, helping usher in a new era of stylish and innovative hotel concepts.

1980-1989

A Decade of Rapid Growth

by Robert Mandelbaum
and Mark Woodworth

In the United States, the 1980s were characterized by significant, turbulent growth in the lodging industry, as an estimated 920,000 hotel rooms opened for a net increase of 40 percent. The economic environment that characterized the early years of the decade reflected a recovery from the turmoil of the late 1970s. High inflation and interest rates led to numerous federal programs, many of which had a significant impact on new construction. The rapid growth in supply provided the opportunity for the leading hotel firms to extend their reach through segmentation. The expanding inventory of hotel rooms led to greater demand for management talent and innovative approaches to profitable operations. The introduction of the revenue management theory late in the decade is perhaps the most important example of this phenomenon.

Like in past cycles, hotel owners rode a volatile roller coaster of business activity during the 1980s, driven both by market conditions and federal policy changes. The latter was particularly true in the areas of tax legislation and banking rules and regulations. The acronym-titled government programs of the 1980s reflect the issues of this decade.

On August 13, 1981, President Ronald Reagan signed into law the Emergency Recovery Tax Act of 1981 (ERTA). The purpose of the bill was to "amend the Internal Revenue Service Code of 1954 to encourage economic growth through reductions in individual income tax rates, the expensing of depreciable property, incentives for small businesses, and incentives for savings." Most of the legislation was aimed at easing the income tax burden on individuals to increase consumer spending. However, ERTA also contained tax incentives that fueled the real estate investment boom of the 1980s that eventually contributed to massive over-development by the end of the decade.

In an effort to assist Savings and Loan (S&L) institutions to compete with banks, the federal government loosened regulations and allowed S&Ls to offer depositors higher interest rates. Attracted by the potential for high returns, S&Ls pooled their resources to offer vast amounts of money to the real estate community. The axiom "Why do developers build? Because they can!" rang true during this period, as hotel developers quickly got in line for these funds, often able to borrow all of the capital required to build their projects. A sharp rise in construction ensued from 1983 to 1988.

Unfortunately, the S&L industry struggled to handle this surge in complex lending activity. Poor market assessment, reliance on untrustworthy appraisals, and corruption all contributed to inadequate underwriting and the approval of loans to projects that were not necessarily market justified, nor financially feasible.

By 1985, the exuberant investment and lending practices of the early part of the decade led to real estate and S&L failures. One year later, Congress passed the Tax Reform Act of

Joe McInerney, now president of AH&LA, then president of Sheraton's franchise division, participates in a radio interview during an AH&MA convention in Vancouver in 1982.

● **Bill Kimpton introduces the "boutique" hotel concept** in the United States with the opening of **Clarion Bedford Hotel** in San Francisco. It features complimentary wine for all guests every day.

● **Le Grand Hôtel Paris** becomes a member of the **Intercontinental** chain.

● The **Accor Group** is born.

● Holiday Inn is the first hotel chain **to offer centralized travel agent commission.**

1980   1981   1982   1983   1984

1986 to eliminate the tax incentives that had artificially spurred real estate development.

In 1989, Congress passed the Federal Institutions Reform, Recovery and Enforcement Act (FIRREA). This act switched control of the S&L industry from the Federal Home Loan Bank Board to the newly created Office of Thrift Supervision. One of the first actions under FIRREA was the setup of the Resolution Trust Corporation (RTC), with the purpose of resolving the hundreds of insolvent S&Ls. During the liquidation process, foreclosed real estate was frequently auctioned off or sold at a significant discount. As of March 1990, the RTC had control over an estimated 158 hotels and 205 resorts that were being prepped for sale. Lodging investors took advantage of the opportunity to increase their portfolios at bargain prices. Some retained their properties, while others made a large profit selling these assets during the prosperous 1990s.

In the '80s, travelers in the United States had their choice of approximately 50,000 hotels offering 2.3 million guest rooms. While the inventory of available lodging facilities was large and branding had fully taken root, there was limited diversity in the rooms and amenities offered. An estimated 54 percent of the 50,000 hotels were moderately priced, full-service properties found along the nation's highways and in the suburbs. Brands like Holiday Inn, Best Western, Ramada, Sheraton, Quality, and Howard Johnson dominated the marketplace, offering consistent, safe accommodation with an all-purpose restaurant, a pool, and a limited amount of meeting space.

Meanwhile, expense-account business travelers and large conventions sought the abundant facilities and services offered by upscale chains such as Hilton, Hyatt, Marriott, and Western International. These larger hotels were frequently situated in cities or airport locations, and offered multiple food and beverage options, as well as large meeting and exhibition spaces. Pricey independent resorts and urban "grand dames" attracted travelers with deep pockets

The main exercise room of the new health club at the Intercontinental in New York included a sauna, steam room, and massage rooms.

In the early 1980s, the American fitness craze led to the development of health clubs in hotels.

- Sheraton becomes the first international hotel chain **to operate a hotel in the People's Republic of China.**

- Randy and Carolyn Smith found **Smith Travel Research (STR) in** Lancaster, Pennsylvania.

- Marriott embraces an innovative **television video checkout system** in its hotels.

- STR launches its **STAR program of custom reports.**

1985   1986   1987   1988   1989

who desired high-end services and amenities. For price-conscious leisure travelers and road warriors, "rooms-only" motels were the preferred choice. While the majority of properties in this category were remnants of small, independent motor courts located on U.S. highways and in rural markets, thousands of economy properties across the nation were affiliated with national chains. The dominant budget brands of the early '80s were Best Value, Days Inn, Motel 6, Red Carpet, La Quinta, and Travelodge.

By 1981, a convergence of changing demographics and advanced market strategies spawned the growth of segmentation in the U.S. lodging industry. Three choices (economy, mid- price, upscale) were not enough to satisfy the expanding desires of travelers, so forward-thinking lodging executives designed a variety of new types of facilities, frequently franchised and/or operated under the same parent hotel company.

Baby boomers comprised approximately 39 percent of the U.S. population in the early 1980s. By the end of the decade, baby boomers were the dominant purchasers of hotel rooms.

Unlike previous generations, the ability and desire to travel became a routine part of life. In addition, women were traveling more than ever, and an estimated 40 percent of all business travelers in 1986 were women. The lodging industry responded to these discerning groups of travelers by developing a variety of niche products, each aimed to match price, facility, and services based on the purpose of the trip and desires of the traveler.

In the '80s, hotel companies continued to expand and segment their product offerings. In an effort to accommodate budget-conscious travelers, hotel companies that historically operated in the moderate-priced, full-service category developed "limited-service" brands that offered comparable guestrooms without the extra food and beverage facilities. These included, the Comfort Inn brand (1981) by Quality Inns and Hampton Inn (1982) by Holiday Inn. In 1983, Marriott, a traditional player in the upscale market, developed Courtyard by Marriott. Hotel brands expanded up the market segment ladder as well. Quality Inns offered franchisees the Quality Royale brand (1981), while Holiday Inns unveiled Crowne Plaza in 1983. Both of these brands were created to appeal to higher-end business, leisure, and group travelers.

Vertical segmentation was not just limited to price categories. Historically, hotel suites were viewed as the exclusive domain of executive business travelers, celebrities, and the affluent. However, in the 1970s, innovative "all-suite" lodging proper-

An artist's rendering of the Sonesta Hotel Beach Club & Casino in Aruba, which opened in 1989.

Randy Smith: Creating a New Standard

by Andrea Morabito

In 1985, Randy Smith had one goal: to create a service to make hotels work better. As a longtime hotel analyst, he saw a need to provide the best information on overall performance trends to the lodging industry and its observers. Smith and his wife, Carolyn, founded Smith Travel Research (STR) that same year, and began to lay the groundwork for what would become the most comprehensive database ever compiled on the hotel industry.

Randy first thought of creating a market share report for the hotel industry when he was working as director of research at Laventhol & Horwath, but each time it was rejected. So he started his own business with a simple plan: to build a database with the names, addresses, and phone numbers of every lodging establishment in the United States. In the beginning, he sold the lists to vendors to use for creating territories for their sales staffs. In 1987, STR received the endorsement of AH&LA, a seal of approval for the young company.

Smith was then contacted by Holiday Inn, which urged him to take his database to the next level and create a market share report. After turning the offer down multiple times, he finally created the Smith Travel Accommodations Report (STAR). In January 1988, STR launched the monthly report with data from 10,000 hotels, measuring each property's market share performance against a self-selected competitive set. Within a few years, every major hotel chain was participating, and the resulting aggregate data revolutionized the way the hotel industry evaluated itself.

Nowadays, STAR tracks nearly 40,000 properties, including those of every major lodging chain. ●

Other Notables

● **Bob Hazard & Gerry Petitt**
In 1981, Bob Hazard and Gerry Petitt's Choice Hotels was the first lodging chain to successfully franchise the economy and mid-priced categories, with the introduction of its Quality Inn and Comfort Inn brands.

● **Bill Kimpton**
Bill Kimpton took hotel development down a different avenue, particularly among the nation's urban centers. He founded San Francisco-based Kimpton Hotels & Restaurants in 1981, thus launching the first collection of boutique hotels. He pioneered the concept by purchasing small, old downtown buildings and converting them into intimate, European-style hotels with personalized guest services and comforting and luxurious amenities.

● **Isadore Sharp**
The 1980s also saw the expansion of Isadore Sharp's Four Seasons brand, well regarded internationally, into the United States. The Toronto-based hotelier entered America by opening flagship properties in a dozen cities across the country during the decade. Soon the hotel company began to shift its business focus to hotel management rather than only property ownership. Over the years, Four Seasons has become noted for its guest services.

ties were introduced and eventually grew into major chains. Granada Royale Hometels offered guests larger guestrooms with discreet sleeping and living areas. Residence Inns added kitchens and dining areas for extended-stay guests.

While suite hotels were born in the 1970s, they grew tremendously in the 1980s. Holiday Inn purchased Granada Royale in 1984 and used it to fuel the growth of its new Embassy Suites brand. Holiday Inn also purchased a portion of Brock Residence Inn in 1985, and the entire Residence Inn brand was eventually sold to Marriott in 1987.

The Educational Institute held a housekeeping seminar in the late 1980s in conjunction with the Colorado and Wyoming Hotel and Motel Association.

As these initial all-suite brands were marketed to consumers seeking an upscale experience, further price-segmentation was observed within the all-suite category. By 1984, Quality Inns had developed the Comfort Suites brand, an all-suite hotel offering moderate prices, with spacious guestrooms featuring separate sleeping and living areas. Suburban Lodge entered the economy all-suite segment in 1987, in an effort to meet the needs of price-sensitive travelers requiring accommodation for an extended period of time.

Meanwhile, the franchise business model employed by many large hotel companies required new and creative ways to grow the revenue derived from royalty payments and other franchise related fees. By offering new products, the franchisers were able to satisfy the demand for additional licenses from their loyal base of franchisees. This helped to keep the franchise fee income streams in-house, as opposed to losing developers to other chains. Further, several markets were becoming saturated with the existing "core" brand hotels. By offering new niche products targeting different types of guests and better serving the evolving preferences of these types of travelers, the franchiser could continue to sell licenses within the same market, without, as the theory went, impacting the existing franchised properties.

By the end of the decade, all-suite hotel rooms represented 5.8 percent of the room inventory at the 25 largest U.S. hotel companies, up from just 0.8 percent in 1980. At the same time, budget and economy rooms grew from 13.2 percent in 1980 to 24 percent in 1990. At the end of the 1980s, terms such as limited-service, all-suite, and extended-stay had become fully entrenched as part of the language of the lodging industry.

Changes within the industry were affecting the operations side of the business as well. The eighth edition of the *Uniform System of Accounts for Hotels (USAH)* was published in 1986, providing expanded formulas and definitions for the growing number of statistics used by hotel managers. This recognition of the

INNOVATIONS

Technology Enhances Guest Expectations

by Sandra Perilli

As airline deregulation made flying more affordable, hotels of the 1980s focused on offering alternative lodging options. With an increase in travelers, the industry needed to differentiate programs, services, and accommodations to gain competitive advantage and win consumer attention. A range of groundbreaking trade innovations soon emerged based on advancing technology and insight analysis collected from target market data.

For the first time, targeted marketing and technology were used to raise the bar on consumer-lodging expectations for the wealthy, as well as the budget conscience. Hotels implemented money saving programs for repeat visitors based on the frequent flier airline concept and offered satisfaction guarantees. Increasing awareness of a healthier lifestyle brought about shared exercise facilities, scenic jogging paths, and golf courses to appeal to the more active travelers. Rights to reserve non-smoking quarters became available, along with an array of hotel restaurant food options ranging from ethnic cuisine to healthy choice menus.

Even the type of in-room amenities offered grew in scope, catering to forgetful travelers and those seeking to be pampered. Rooms were pre-stocked with hairdryers, irons, disposable personal items, and waiting bathrobes. Doorfront newspaper delivery became popular, Pay-Per-View television was accessible, and speedy video checkout (via the room's television) helped visitors avoid long front desk lines.

In addition to new programs and amenities, hotels of the '80s also recognized the needs of families with children. The appearance of resorts and casinos allowed adults to indulge in gambling, sunning, working out, and dining, while kids spent a day with counselors playing games, enjoying crafts, and meeting others their age. ●

1982
● **Marriott International** introduced the hotel industry's first program rewarding **frequent visitors**. Frequent-stay reward programs would take off in popularity shotrly thereafter.

1983
● **Westin began accepting major credit cards** to book reservations and at checkout.

● The first **optical electronic keycard** was developed by VingCard.

1984
● Hotels started to develop the **non-smoking room concept**.

1986
● **Room reservations** via connected hotel desks were implemented by **Days Inn**.

● **Teledex Corporation** offered the first hotel phone built for lodging accommodations.

1989
● Hyatt introduced a program for children's activities nationwide, opened a business center at the **Hyatt Regency Chicago**.

increased use of statistical analysis was a precursor to the explosion that would begin by the end of the decade. In January 1988, Smith Travel Research launched its STAR program of custom reports that allowed individual hotels and chains to measure their market share. Armed with aggregated supply, demand and revenue data from tens of thousands of hotels across the country, individual hotel managers, chain developers, owners, lenders, consultants and analysts were provided with a consistent source of data that allowed them to evaluate historical performance and provide a solid basis for future actions. Terminology such as competitive set, fair share, yield, and market penetration are now commonplace in the industy.

As roadside motor centers grew in popularity, chains such as Hampton Inn thrived during the 1980s.

Guest safety and security was also an important industry topic in this decade. In November 1980, a tragic fire at the MGM Grand Hotel and Casino (now Bally's) in Las Vegas resulted in the death of 87 people. This event generated increased awareness of hotel fire safety and security procedures and policies. Resulting legislation is the reason why hotels now post floor maps and emergency evacuation procedure instructions on the back of every hotel door found in the United States.

Another area that had a dramatic impact on the hotel industry was telecommunications, as long-distance telephone service was partially deregulated in 1984. This allowed hotels to resell telephone services, along with a surcharge, and separate telephone departments were created. While hotels initially showed slight profits, hotel guests began to flock to lobby pay phones and use their personal calling card in an effort to avoid the surcharge. Hotel literature explaining these often-complex charges were the precursor to the current movement toward full disclosure of fees charged by many hotels today.

After growing substantially in the 1970s and early 1980s, energy costs were separated from the operations and maintenance department in 1986. In addition, departmental schedules were developed within the administrative and general (A&G) department in recognition of the increased importance of data processing and human resources. Another change within A&G was the movement of management fees into a separate line item on the statement of income.

An innovation adopted from the airline industry that marked a turning point for hotels was the implementation of enhanced revenue, or "yield" management practices. Led by pioneering efforts of Bob Cross, yield management strives to maximize revenue and/or profits by influencing consumer behavior through pricing. Managers began to evaluate and adjust room rates based on historical and projected booking patterns. 100th

Assassination Attempt Leads to Changes in Law

by Treanna Santillo

As the 1980s unfolded, it brought with it an event that has gone down in American history: the attempted assassination of the 40th president of the United States, Ronald Reagan. On March 30th, 1981, just 69 days into his presidency, President Reagan was leaving a luncheon at the Washington Hilton Hotel when he was shot by John Hinckley, Jr.

Arriving a day before, on March 29th, Hinckley checked into the Park Central Hotel in Washington, D.C., and upon learning the president's schedule through the media, planned his attack. As later told by Hinckley, the reason behind the shooting was to impress actress Jodie Foster with the enormity of his actions.

Minutes before 2:30 in the afternoon, President Reagan emerged from the Washington Hilton to be greeted by the sound of gunshots. As Hinckley separated himself from the crowd, he fired six shots within three seconds, injuring several people.

James Brady, the White House press secretary, was one victim who suffered severe trauma, leading to a permanent disability. Upon recovering, Brady fought to enact tougher gun control laws and to reduce gun violence within the United States. In addition to Brady, a Secret Service agent and police officer also sustained injuries due to the shooting.

Seconds after the shooting, Secret Service agents rushed Reagan away from the scene, where it was initially thought he had not been hurt.

On June 21, 1982, Hinckley was found not guilty due to reason of insanity, as a result of psychiatric reports produced by the defense. Although a dismal verdict, as felt by many Americans, it led Congress, along with many states, to rewrite laws on insanity defense. Three states have since abolished it. Hinckley showed no signs of guilt for his actions and remains a patient at Saint Elizabeths Hospital in Washington, D.C. ●

1985

● **The Plaza Accord is signed**

In the 1980s it was evident that serious changes to foreign policy were needed, as previous methods to normalize foreign currency failed, leaving currency regulation to simple supply and demand. These unfavorable conditions led to the Plaza Accord, when on September 22, 1985, members of the G5 nations, including the United States, Japan, West Germany, the United Kingdom, and France, met to resolve the problem at the Plaza Hotel in New York City.

1986

● **Al Capone's Vault Opened**

Al Capone was a notorious 1920s gangster who resided in Chicago, Illinois. In July 1928, Capone moved his headquarters to the Lexington Hotel in Chicago, where he carried out his various 'businesses' until his arrest in 1931. About 50 years later, major renovations at the Lexington Hotel inadvertently led to an astounding discovery. The construction company uncovered secret tunnels Capone had previously set up for fast getaways from the police. Rumors started circling that Capone also hid a vault under the hotel, and newscaster Geraldo Rivera decided to host a live TV special exposing the vault's contents. However, the vault only contained items such as dirt, empty bottles, and a tub possibly used to create moonshine.

Though controversial when built in the '80s, the Marriott Marquis became a focal point of the revitalized Times Square in the 1990s.

1990-1999

A Wired New World

by Cheryl-Anne Sturken

The U.S. hotel industry is a restless one. And at no time in the 1990s, a decade marked with astonishing global change and innovation, did it seem content to stand still, if even for a moment. On the larger world stage, the North American Free Trade Agreement was signed into law by President Bill Clinton; and Nelson Mandela, the former leader of South Africa's African National Congress, was released from jail after 30 years of imprisonment. Hong Kong was handed over to the People's Republic of China after 155 years of British colonial rule, and the European Union was formed. On U.S. soil, the New York Yankees closed the decade by steamrolling the Atlanta Braves to win their 25th World Series title in 1999.

It was during this decade that the hotel industry emerged as a major economic player with a strong, cohesive voice. In those 10 years, new hotel companies were established and chains launched, groundbreaking technologies became mainstream amenities, and a new selling platform — the Internet — changed the relationship between hotel management and guests forever. Not surprisingly, as the economic engine of the hotel industry grew in size and clout, AH&MA found its role on Capitol Hill as the voice for the industry to be an increasingly important and vocal one.

Bill Marriott, chairman and CEO of Marriott International, addresses a gathering of AH&MA.

In 1991, with the Gulf War and the accompanying recession finally over, hotel companies were eager to get back to the business of profit-making. There was, however, an awful lot of fence mending to do. Over the previous six years, as demand plummeted, the industry had lost billions of dollars. The average room rate hovered at just $58.70, and occupancy was a mere 64 percent. Resiliency, however, is another well-honed lodging industry trait. By the end of 1992, hotel companies were back in the black, and the industry was well on track to establishing record-high profit margins, thanks largely in part to increased demand, rising room rates that outpaced inflation, and tighter operating cost controls. By 1997, the industry was at the top of its game, churning out a net profit of $17 billion, more than that of the previous 10 years combined. Even more impressive, PKF Hospitality Research reported that between 1991 to 2000, U.S. hotels improved their profitability margins an average of 11.4 percent per year — 4.5 percent times the rate of inflation.

During the first half of the 1990s, as hotel companies focused their attention on increasing productivity and profitability, they employed an aggressive acquisition-based growth strategy that fueled a rapid portfolio expansion for many of the industry's key players. Announcements of major mergers and acquisitions were practically a daily occurrence, and keeping track of who owned whom, or even daring to speculate, in the decade's fast-moving real estate investment market could have brought even the

● **The Gulf War begins** and there is great insecurity for both individuals and businesses. Hoteliers were forced to become more creative in finding ways of attracting guests.

● Hospitality Franchise Systems launches with the acquisition of Days Inn. **It would become part of Cendant Corporation in 1997.**

● Radisson is first to offer **business-class rooms.**

● **The Marriott Company splits** into Marriott International and Host Marriott Corporation.

1990   **1991**   **1992**   **1993**   **1994**

most seasoned Monopoly players to their knees.

In 1990, Accor bought out the Dallas-based Motel 6 chain for $1.3 billion, giving the French-owned company entree into the U.S. economy-hotel sector. In 1996, Doubletree Corporation bought Red Lion Hotels for $1.2 billion, only to be snapped up the following year by Memphis, Tennessee-based Promus Hotel Corporation (which included Embassy Suites and Hampton Suites) for $4 billion. A few years later in 1999, Doubletree became part of Hilton Hotels' portfolio, when the then Beverly Hills, California-based chain under the leadership of Stephen Bollenbach, president and chief executive officer, acquired Promus in a deal worth $3.7 billion in cash and stock. Three years earlier, in June 1996, and just four months after jumping to Hilton from The Walt Disney Company, Bollenbach had inked a deal acquiring Bally Entertainment Group for $3 billion. With six casino hotels under its belt, Hilton suddenly found itself holding the title of the world's largest casino-gaming company.

In 1997, a particularly robust year at the deal table, several established chains changed hands. In early February, Bethesda, Maryland-based Marriott International — now leaner after a decisive restructuring plan in 1993 that split Marriott Corporation into Host Marriott and Marriott International — acquired the Renaissance brand for $1 billion and immediately set about investing billions in repositioning the brand globally. Four years later, it added 46 hotels under the Renaissance flag, expanding the brand's global portfolio to 114. Chairman and chief executive officer, J. Willard Marriott, Jr. (Bill Marriott), however, was not finished. Missing from Marriott International's extensive chain portfolio, one that spanned from limited-service to high-end, full-service brands, was an established luxury product, one with iconic status and emotional cache. Not for long, though.

In 1997 the company acquired a 49 percent controlling interest in the storied, but financially strapped, Ritz-Carlton Hotel Company for $200 million in cash and assumed debt. The following year, on the heels of several

During the 1990s, hotel companies such as Mandarin-Oriental took lobby designs to new heights.

In 1997, the lodging industry's net profit of $17 billion was more than the previous 10 years combined.

● **Starwood** Hotels and Resorts launches.

● Marriott acquires **the Ritz-Carlton Hotel Company LLC**.

● **Kimpton is first in the industry to develop "tall rooms"** to accommodate taller guests at Fifth Avenue Suites in Portland, Oregon, and other properties throughout the country.

● **Marriott acquires the Renaissance Hotel Group** and introduces TownePlace Suites, Fairfield Suites, and the Marriott Executive Residences brands.

● Starwood Hotels & Resorts Worldwide acquires **the Sheraton brand**.

● Westin debuts the **Heavenly Bed**, creating a surge of improvements in bedding.

1995   1996   1997   1998   1999

high-profile buyouts of a handful of Ritz-Carlton properties, Marriott owned the chain outright. Over the course of the next 12 years, with founding president and chief operating officer Horst Schultze at the helm, Ritz-Carlton emerged as one of the hotel industry's most recognizable brands, going head-to-head with its Canadian competitor, Four Seasons Hotel Company, for worldwide luxury dominance.

Another hotel company making big strides in 1990s was White Plains, New York-based Starwood Lodging, a then fledgling startup hotel company founded in 1995 by Barry S. Sternlicht, a nimble investor with a penchant for fast-paced, no-holds barred real estate deals and access to the deep pockets of a handful of wealthy investors to help make them happen. In 1997, Starwood made two major acquisitions that set it on a projectile growth course: the purchase of Westin Hotels & Resorts for $1.8 billion and ITT Sheraton Corporation (which included Four Points by Sheraton, Sheraton and the Luxury Collection) for $14.3 billion. By February of 1998, with both deals finalized, the renamed Starwood Hotels & Resorts Worldwide included

four brands with a combined portfolio of 650 hotels and resorts in more than 70 countries worldwide — impressive by any start-up standards. Like Marriott, however, Starwood was not content to rest. In December 1998, the company launched its revolutionary W boutique brand, with the opening of the 720-room W New York at the corner of 49th Street and Lexington Avenue. The following year, it opened five more Ws; two more in New York City, and one each in Atlanta, San Francisco, and Seattle.

While the art of the mega-real estate hotel deal was surely honed in the 1990s, there was much more to this decade than feverish consolidation. Once their portfolios were in place, hotel companies turned their attention to pushing the envelope on architectural design and setting the bar ever higher on in-room amenities and service standards. In a nod to the growing numbers of road warriors, and their importance to the bottom line, Minneapolis, Minnesota-based Radisson Hotels Worldwide introduced business class guestrooms in 1993. The guestrooms included special amenities such as larger bath areas, in-room coffee makers, and complimentary breakfast. With it, life on the road for the masses of weary business travelers was transformed from daily grind to downright glamorous. It was an innovation that Radisson's competitors rushed to emulate. Over the following decade, the concept became mainstream in hotel design and evolved to include entire floors dedicated to business travelers, featuring private lounges staffed by concierges, complimentary

Companies such as Loews Hotels & Resorts created community settings in lobbies during the 1990s.

Marilyn Carlson Nelson:
Changing the Meaning of Leader

by Alex Corini

Marilyn Carlson Nelson has been ranked by _Forbes_ magazine as one of "The World's 100 Most Powerful Women," and was CEO of the largest company in the world run by a female. Considering that she was asked to use her initials at her first job as a security analyst, Carlson Nelson has definitely come a long way in the business world.

Born in Minneapolis, Minnesota, Carlson Nelson inherited the leadership qualities prevalent in her family. She joined the Carlson Companies 1965 (still called the Gold Bond Stamp Company until 1973) as regional representative.

She was appointed director of community relations in 1968, then senior vice president in 1989, and eventually vice chair in 1991.

To prove the status quo of the day wrong, she followed in her father's footsteps and influenced nearly every facet of Carlson Companies (the parent company of the Radisson hotel chain and TGIFriday restaurants, to name a few). Her father, Curtis Carlson, started the Gold Bond Stamp Company with a $55 loan. Carlson Nelson expanded upon her father's vision and steered the company to new horizons. When she became CEO in 1998, she finally had the opportunity to reshape what it meant to do business with Carlson Companies.

From the beginning, she exemplified a different kind of leadership. At her first meeting as CEO, it is said that she rolled up to the podium on rollerblades, quickly gaining the attention of other top brass, as well as the entire industry. Under her guidance, the company expanded into business travel, marketing, and cruise lines, and more important, doubled its profit. Today, the company employs more than 190,000 people worldwide. Carlson Nelson was a member of the International Business Council of the World Economic Forum, and later was appointed chair of the National Women's Business Council by President George W. Bush.

But it is not just the business world that recognizes her achievements. She holds the Woodrow Wilson Award for Corporate Citizenship for being active in furthering her community — she played an integral role in bringing the Super Bowl to Minneapolis in 1992. She still continues to bring ingenuity to her industry, while redefining what it means to be a leader. ●

Other Notables

● **Barry Sternlicht**
When it comes to hotels, Barry Sternlicht's expertise is unparalleled. As the leader of Starwood Hotels and Resorts, his influence is seen throughout the company's notable brands, including Westin, W, and Sheraton.

● **Ian Schrager**
Ian Schrager's unique idea of the upscale boutique hotel drastically influenced design and architecture within the lodging industry. As the co-owner of the infamous Studio 54 in the 1970s, Schrager's often volatile career shifted to the hospitality world in the '80s with the re-opening of the stunningly designed Paramount and Royalton hotels in New York City.

all-day food and beverage, and a host of destination-unique offerings.

The boutique concept, which revolutionized the hospitality industry during the previous decade, was still very much in its infancy. During the

Kimpton Hotels & Resorts continued to open new hotels, gaining a reputation for its enivronmental consciousness.

Launched in the 1980s, the boutique concept exploded in the 1990s.

1990s, however, the concept hit its stride, as increasing numbers of travelers embraced the notion of boutique hotels as a distinct category. Leading the way were two hotel visionaries, Ian Schrager and Bill Kimpton, whose design-driven hotels defied the conventionality of chain consistency by placing a premium on individuality.

Schrager, who had opened the very chic and trendy Royalton in New York City in 1988, teamed up with well-known designer Phillipe Starck, on the Paramount in the heart of New York City's Times Square district, followed by the Delano in Miami's South Beach. Both projects turned the industry on its ear with the concept of

"lobby socializing" as central to a hotel's identity. This previously overlooked public space became each hotel's center of energy, lively social hubs with multiple bars, restaurants, and alcoves where guests wanted to linger and soak up the experience, rather than rush back to the privacy of their guestrooms.

While Schrager focused on reinventing the lobby, Kimpton, head of San Francisco, California-based Kimpton Hotels & Restaurants, focused on delivering chef-driven restaurants at his boutique properties. It was a concept that the larger chains would not get around to for almost another decade. In another industry milestone in 1995, he launched Hotel Monaco, the first boutique chain. The first to open was the Hotel Monaco San Francisco, featuring the French-themed restaurant, the Grand Café. Fifteen years later, the chain would number nine hotels. Sadly, Bill Kimpton passed away in 2001, but a "tree of life" dedicated to his memory graces the lobby of the first Hotel Monaco.

Meanwhile, Las Vegas, Nevada, was embracing a hotel design trend all its own, one where size, theme, and excess became the new code words in hotel architecture. Over the course of the decade, the arrival of several multimillion-dollar, mega-resorts transformed the strip into a round-the-clock, three-dimensional entertainment destination. When it opened on June 19, 1990, the 4,032-room Excalibur Hotel & Casino was the world's largest resort. Two years later, it would lose that title to the 5,005-

The Rebirth of Ingenuity

by Joy Guermont

Although the 1990s were a time of change and unrest for the hotel industry, it was also a decade of rebirth. In the early '90s, growth halted as overbuilding in the '80s, coupled with the economic recession of the time, forced a number of hotels to close, sell at devaluated

prices, or fall victim to hostile takeover. With an over-abundance of rooms, the United States' consumers spending at a low mark, and the Gulf War of 1991 curtailing international travel, some hotel rooms lay empty. However, by the mid '90s ingenuity was on the rise, the economy leveled out and the hotel industry saw a revival.

Both nationally and internationally, smaller chains and individually owned hotels were frequently catching the eye of larger investment groups. Companies continued to diversify by creating greater delineations between hotel chains, and began to market themselves to specific segments — such as destination or business, budget or luxury. Major franchising companies, such as Cendant Corporation (eventually, Wyndham Hotels & Resorts), continued to invest in the U.S. market, acquiring mid-level hotel brands, as new chains were organized, reflagged, built and sold.

Catering to business travelers by offering amenities such as voicemail, faxing, computer access, and larger rooms was an initial step in creating enhanced guest services. Marketing concepts such as frequent guest programs were also becoming more common. An increase in demand for these services led to business class suites being built with living areas, kitchenettes, and bedrooms. Hotels re-formed their layouts by adding conference rooms, business centers, and areas to relax or exercise. In this decade, the extended-stay hotel concept further flourished. By 1998, these long-stay, business-oriented properties became so popular that 40 percent of rooms planned for construction were set within this "extended-stay" style.

As the industry began to regain its ground, hotels went to new heights to elevate the customer's experience. In 1993 in New York City, the Four Seasons introduced the city's "new tallest hotel" that featured window blinds that could be raised and lowered by a switch, bathtubs that filled in a minute's time, and TVs in the bathrooms. Further advancements in everyday amenities and services, such as check-in and reservations, improved as computers and software programs became more advanced and accessible. ●

1990

● **Westin** was the first hotel to provide **voice mail service** to guests.

1992

● **Choice Hotels** became the **largest franchise hotel chain** in the world.

1994

● The first online hotel catalog was launched at **www.travelweb.com**.

● **Hyatt** and **Promus** were the first hotels to introduce **Web sites**.

1995

● **Choice Hotels** and **Promus** offered guests "real time" access to a central reservations systems.

● **Choice Hotels** and **Holiday Inn** launched **Internet booking** for guests.

room MGM Grand Hotel. For sheer design force, the Luxor, a 30-story high pyramid of black glass, is one of the city's most recognizable symbols. Designed by architect Veldon Simpson, the ancient Egyptian-themed

PHOTO COURTESY OF THE LAS VEGAS NEWS BUREAU

The 1990s were a boom time for Las Vegas as new resorts, such as the Bellagio, were built quickly.

hotel, which opened its doors in 1993, is viewed as one of the finest examples of post-modern architecture. But it is developer Steve Wynn, arguably one of the hotel industry's greatest creators of spectacle, who took lavishness on the strip to a new level, with the opening of the Bellagio in 1998. Designed by architect Jon Jerde, the luxury resort featured a museum-quality art gallery, a conservatory and botanical gardens, high-end retail boutiques, and outdoor fountains choreographed to music. At a cost of $1.7 billion, it was the world's most expensive hotel.

No event, however, had as significant and altering affect on the lodging industry as the rise of e-commerce.

Starting in the mid-1990s, airlines began selling directly to the consumer over the Internet via online travel companies. It was not long before hotels hitched their star to the concept. By 1999, with growing numbers of consumers warming to the thrill of their own buying power, travel was the largest e-commerce category and hotel room sales on the Internet were more than $1 billion. By 2002 that number would skyrocket to $6.3 billion. The growing shift to online hotel room sales and the intense competition it sparked across the industry forced hotels to rethink their marketing strategies. Because, for the first time consumers had transparency in comparison shopping — from room rate and on-site amenities.

One of the most important challenges to the industry came early in the decade, when on July 26, 1990 the Americans with Disabilities Act (ADA) was signed into law by President George H. W. Bush. As the industry's regulatory and guiding voice, AH&MA expressed its commitment to this landmark legislation, which prohibited discrimination on the basis of disability and urged its members to take a common-sense approach to ensuring compliance. Over the course of the decade, hotels would spend billions of dollars ensuring their facilities were accessible to individuals with disabilities, often investing in upgrades to their properties to adhere to the regulations. They would, also, however, spend millions of dollars defending themselves against "drive-by" lawsuits brought by individuals and groups. 100th

Technology in the Spotlight for Y2K

by Joy Guermont

It is the unperceivable or disastrous that eludes us while booking accommodations for vacation or business, and yet when something out of the ordinary strikes we still expect the luxuries to which we are accustomed.

The approaching second millennium sent panic racing through the minds of many people around the world as a two-digit catastrophe threatened a global plague. Not only were personal possessions at stake, but also the entire infrastructure as a nation was sure to fail. As individuals withdrew savings from bank accounts, credit cards expiring in the year 2000 were denied, and fear grew.

Faulty date logic or century date change was programmed years before to conserve limited and expensive computer memory. Replacing computers or software seemed the simplest of solutions, but the true obstacle lay within "embedded systems." These time and date sequences controlled microwaves, utilities, even subways — and many believed their collapse would enact an unimaginable chain of events.

While the Y2K bug had unexpectedly swarmed down upon the masses, it crept slowly into the world of business. By the mid-1990s, hotels were already spending millions of dollars and thousands of hours on research teams and new technology. Starwood Hotels & Resorts organized pertinent information and made it accessible to the entire industry. By June 1996, it had already reserved rooms into the year 2000. Hyatt developed formal processes to test a multitude of systems, ranging from software to elevators. When the ball dropped in Times Square, and the world continued to spin, those who were brave enough to reserve the date and venture out, enjoyed a night's celebration that was 2000 years in the making. And they did so without a disruption of comfort or service. ●

1993

● **Blizzard blankets Eastern U.S.**
In March 1993, the "Storm of the Century" had a devastating impact on the eastern United States. More than 130 million people witnessed the storm and many were left stranded on roadsides, in airports, or within their homes without heat and electricity. The extreme weather drove people to the safety and warmth of hotels. A number of East Coast hotels reserved rooms for their staff in order to remain open and functioning. During this state of emergency, the hospitality industry provided countless people with the essential needs for survival. Shelter alone must have felt like a luxury.

1997

● **Princess Diana Dines at the Ritz**
On August 31, 1997, Diana, Princess of Wales, dined with companion Dodi Al-Fayed at the Hotel Ritz Paris, a place known for hosting world-famous personalities through the years, including legendary author Ernest Hemingway and British Prime Minister Winston Churchill. Later that evening, the world would be shocked to hear of their deaths as the result of a car accident said to be caused when their driver sped away from the hotel and through the city in an attempt to flee a horde of chasing paparazzi.

In the middle of the decade Starwood Hotels & Resorts released plans for the new aloft brand.

2000-2009

Of Upswings and Downturns

by Corey Limbach

The first decade of the 21st century has had no shortage of creativity and progress within the hotel industry. Yet this period has also been one in which outside forces impacted the industry in numerous ways, and forced hotel developers, owners, and operators to react to these sweeping societal changes.

The new millennium arrived as the United States was in the midst of a tremendous economic boom fueled by the increasing presence of the Internet in the commerce system. Sales over the Internet — or e-commerce — were growing by double digits annually and this fueled a boom in high technology stocks that saw the markets grow to unprecedented levels. Although Federal Reserve Chairman Alan Greenspan warned of "irrational exuberance" in the markets in 1996, the growth had continued and in 2000 was at its highest levels. The dot-com bubble peaked on March 10, 2000, with the NASDAQ composite index peaking at 5,048.62.

By the end of 2000 and into 2001, the bubble had burst and the economy was slowing. Then, on September 11, 2001, the terrorist attacks on New York City and Washington, D.C., occurred, casting a shadow over the entire decade. The events of 9/11 had broad consequences for the entire nation and the world, and, like every-

Many hotel companies set out to modernize their iconic properties during the current decade, such as with Holiday Inn's vast rebranding.

one else, the hotel industry felt them immediately. In the aftermath of 9/11, air travel in the United States decreased dramatically as travelers feared a reprise of the terrorists' methods of hijacking commercial aircraft. While airline passenger traffic eventually recovered throughout the decade, the consequences of the attacks can still be felt in the form of new security measures that have changed the perceived ease of air travel.

The combined impact of the events of 9/11 and the bursting of the dot-com bubble begat an economic downturn, and the lodging markets fell from their peak performance of 2000. In the midst of this downturn, the emerging online hotel booking companies began to gain traction with travelers of all types. These companies took advantage of the fact that despite the crash of technology stocks, Internet usage continued to grow by leaps and bounds. Whereas in 1999 approximately 24 percent of people in the developed world were Internet users, by 2004 this had more than doubled to 54 percent. Interestingly, these Internet users increasingly turned to travel sites for their trip planning.

The increase in online reservations paralleled the growth of Internet use, as Internet booking of hotel rooms grew to nearly half of all hotel bookings during the decade. Another online phenomenon that emerged at this time was the rise in online travel and hotel reviews by individual customers. Web sites such as TripAdvisor.com, a travel information social networking site, was launched in 2000, and boasted more than 25 million unique monthly visitors in 2008.

● Marriott, Hyatt, InterContinental Hotels Group, and ClubCorp found purchasing consortium **Avendra**.

● AH&MA changes its name to the **American Hotel & Lodging Association (AH&LA)**.

● In the aftermath of **9/11**, the travel industry sees one of its worst downturns ever.

American Hotel & Lodging Association

● **Intercontinental Hotels Group** debuts **Hotel Indigo**, the first retail-industry inspired lodging brand characterized by integrated design features.

| 2000 | 2001 | 2002 | 2003 | 2004 |

At the same time as hotel companies were battling to maximize the benefits of the emerging Internet technology, another front emerged that took them back to basics. The guestroom bed, a feature that is so elemental to what constitutes a hotel room, had been largely ignored for years — until in August, 1999, when Starwood Hotels & Resorts debuted the Heavenly Bed in its Westin properties. Research showed that Heavenly Beds were a key contributor to the brand's overall satisfaction ratings, and allowed its properties to charge premiums for guestrooms. Soon, other hotel chains were forced to follow suit. Thus were born the "bed wars," with Hilton launching its Suite Dreams bed, Crowne Plaza introducing its Sleep Advantage system, and Hyatt promoting its Grand Bed, among others. The chains mandated replacing all of the beds in their systems, and millions were spent annually on new bedding throughout the industry.

These bedding programs did not just consist of new high-quality mattresses, but also included fine-quality, high-thread-count linens, triple-sheeting for extra comfort, and several types of pillows to create a complete comfort package. Some hotels went to the extreme of having a pillow menu so guests could choose between down or foam, firm or soft, and other choices. Furthermore, the bedding became such an integral part of the hotel chains' marketing that they began to sell their bedding systems to guests at retail, and by early 2009 Westin reported selling 30,000 of its beds.

In keeping with the renewed emphasis on the comfort and style of the bedding in their rooms, the brands began to incorporate other elements of residential style into their designs. By the middle portion of the decade, the economy had begun to improve and a major driving force was the rise in the national housing markets. Climbing real estate values allowed homeowners to live an increasingly luxurious lifestyle, and these consumers began to expect the same level of style and comfort in the hotels.

Such heighted expectations led to a proliferation of new brands in the market, as companies sought to stake

Nowadays, hotels are going green. Some brands, such as Element, are striving for LEED certification brandwide.

In 2006, Cendant Corporation spun off its lodging business, to create Wyndham Worldwide.

● **Westin** and **Marriott** announce that all of their hotels in Canada and the United States are **non-smoking** buildings.

● **GAIA Napa Valley Hotel &Spa** is opened as the **first LEED Gold hotel** in the United States.

2005   2006   2007   2008   2009

111

their claim as the brand that not only fit but also defined the lifestyle of their guests. PricewaterhouseCoopers reported that between 2005 and 2007, 34 new brands were launched

Known as the Riot House in the 1970s, Hyatt turned the infamous property into Andaz West Hollywood. These days, no TVs are seen flying out of its windows.

in the United States, an astonishing number not seen since the brand boom of the late 1980s. Several of the mainstream brands, such as aloft & Element (by Starwood Hotels) and Hyatt Place (by Hyatt Hotels Corporation) incorporated aspects of modern and residential style. Even Marriott

surprised the industry in 2007 by announcing a partnership with the icon of modern hotel style and boutique hotel development, Ian Schrager, launching the Edition brand.

More than half of the brands introduced during this period were at the luxury level, and these concepts merged upscale branding with one of the other dominant trends of the period, the increasing prominence of the condo hotel. Condo hotels have existed since the 1970s, but for many years they had not been a significant component of hotel real estate, as developers did not want to register their projects as securities with the SEC. In 2002, however, the SEC issued a "no action" letter to Intrawest indicating that as long as the marketing of the rental program was kept strictly separate from the marketing of the condominium units, they would not need to register as a security. This and other similar rulings opened the door for developers to adopt the selling of condos as a strategy for financing their other hotel projects.

The Educational Institute's Lodging Management Program Competition helps teach high school students the real-life workings of hotels.

Jonathan Tisch:
The Art of Enjoyable Environments

by Alex Corini

Other Notables

● **Bill Marriott**

John Willard "Bill" Marriott Jr. joined his father's Marriott Corporation in 1956, holding many executive positions, leading up to his position as CEO in 1972. As an industry icon and renowned hospitality professional, he is on the executive committee of the World Travel & Tourism Council and National Business Council.

● **Harris Rosen**

In the mid 1970s, the Orlando hotel industry was in a rut until Harris Rosen (voted Orlando's "2006 Corporate Citizen of the Year" for his philanthropy) came along. After some innovative marketing techniques, his company now owns seven Orlando properties and employs more than 3,000 people.

How do you create a successful luxury hotel chain? Jonathan Tisch seems to have the answer — by "empowering your employees" and "encouraging partnerships." Tisch, the chairman and CEO of Loews Hotels, as well as a member of the office of the president of Loews Corporation, has been enhancing his luxury hotels by creating an enjoyable environment for customers, as well as his employees.

Tisch was born in 1953 in Scarsdale, New York. His father started the Loews company with his brother, Laurence Tisch, and Jonathan would often spend time at one of the family's hotels, helping behind the front desk.

Tisch did whatever he could to sharpen his leadership skills. While attending college at Tufts University, he headed the Tufts Concert Board, which was responsible for putting on shows with such acts as Stevie Wonder and Billy Joel — an impressive feat for any college student. After graduating, he worked in multiple facets of television production. For his work, he received two local Emmy Awards nominations. He returned to New York City and the travel industry in 1979.

Since Tisch took over Loews Hotels in 1989, he has implemented many key strategies that have helped the chain grow. His "community-centered" focus on business is considered instrumental in the modern development of the hospitality industry. He oversees 19 of his company's hotels, with locations in Miami Beach, Los Angeles, and Montreal. Tisch is also the chairman of the Travel Business Roundtable.

Believing that the best way to create a successful company is through community involvement, Tisch is also a philanthropist. He has made notable donations to numerous organizations, including The College of Citizenship and Public Service, located at Tufts University. At his company, Tisch has led many initiatives, including the Minority Business Enterprise Program, which gives minority and women-owned businesses the opportunity to partner with the company. He has also made Loews environmentally responsible and created extensive recycling programs. ●

With the rising residential values nationally and the aging of the baby boomer population, the economics and demographics were ripe for this type of development. Condo hotels, where all or a portion of the units in a hotel are owned individually and operated as a hotel, with the individual owners receiving a split of the income generated, became a driving force in new development in the mid-2000s. Another subset of the condo hotel development boom, particularly in the luxury market, was the inclusion of a residential component within a large hotel project. Developers found that residential condos that received services from the hotel, and were affiliated with a well-known luxury brand such as Ritz-Carlton, Four Seasons, or the Trump Hotel Collection sold at strong premiums over standard condominiums. Given the high cost of development and the growing appetite for residential real estate, there were few large hotels or resorts developed in the decade that did not include some form of residential component.

The first decade of the new millennium closes on a challenging note, however. And the condo hotel market is no exception. Beginning in 2007, as the residential real estate market began to show cracks, and newer projects began to run into difficulty achieving sales goals. Several high-profile projects were halted after construction had already begun, signaling the troubles within the markets. While the condo hotel trend may pick up again once the nation's housing market regains some sort of equilibrium, it remains to be seen whther it will again reach the dizzying levels seen in the middle of this decade.

Additionally, the condo hotel market may have been the first segment of the industry to feel the effects of the burst housing bubble, but the collapse of the residential markets eventually had wide repercussions throughout the nation's economy. Whereas the nation's economy and lodging market entered the decade at the peak of the dot-com bubble, it is ending the decade in the midst of a major economic recession. The collapse of the financial markets had a rapid and profound effect on the hotel markets. Both business and leisure travel nose-dived in the latter half of 2008 and into 2009, but perhaps the hardest hit market segment has been the group market. With the federal bailout of several large banks and insurance giant AIG, increased scrutiny on corporate spending mushroomed into wholesale criticism of the "lavish excess" of conferences held at luxury or upscale hotels or resorts. As a result, even strong companies which had no connection to the bailout started to cancel or curtail group meetings across the world — in what has become known as the "AIG effect." In response, the industry has

Extended-stay properties continue to flourish, as evidenced by the opening of the 100th Staybridge Suites.

The Impact of the Internet

by Marla Cimini

Technology has continued to impact the hospitality industry throughout the current decade, as the growth and popularity of the Internet and online services have played an ongoing role in hospitality innovation. With its enhanced speed and accessibility, the Internet has opened a bright new cyberworld to travelers, thus providing an easy way to access hotel information, book rooms, and share opinions — with the simple click of a mouse.

Online reservations have skyrocketed since the early 2000s, as Web site bookings increased to nearly half of all those made through central reservation systems (CRS). Nowadays, hotel companies are creating their own online booking sites to show travelers easy ways to find and compare hotel values across the globe in a matter of minutes.

Another online trend that emerged during the decade was the rapid rise in social networking, which allows travelers to instantly post their experiences and reviews with others around the world through immediate photo and video sharing. Ongoing research indicates that user-generated content has a strong influence on consumer behavior, and social media outlets, as well as hotels, have continued to enhance their sites and attract more consumers. Most recently, the continuing rise of social networking has presented new opportunities for operators to reach customers, while aggregator Web sites (which search multiple sites to identify the best travel deals) provide travelers with even more avenues to hunt for good travel bargains.

Today, hotels everywhere use blogs, online newsletters, Twitter updates, Facebook messages, and more to communicate with guests via the Internet and promote their properties around the world. Mobile technology is also playing an increasingly important role as well, as devotees of "smart phones," get their travel information on the go. In fact, Apple's ubiquitous iPhone offers a seemingly infinite roster of applications designed for easy travel, offering everything from hotel locators, to language translators, to flight information, and tipping guides. ●

2000

● **Trip Advisor** was launched.

● **Travelocity,** although introduced in the mid-90s, became a public company and establishes itself as the **"go-to" reservation site for travelers around the world.**

2002

● **Hotel Technology Next Generation (HTNG) was founded** as a non-profit global trade association serving hotel companies and technology providers.

2004

● **Smith Travel Research** created Global Lodging Review (now Global Hotel Review) to help hoteliers keep an eye on industry trends and statistics.

2007

● **Apple's iPhone was launched.** Fans of smartphones embrace the many travel "apps." **Choice Hotels was the first hotel company** to create a specific app for the device.

2008

● **Flat-panel TVs became commonplace in hotel rooms** across the USA and begin to perform addition room control functions other than entertainment.

formed Keep America Meeting in association with the U.S. Travel Association to promote the economic benefits of the meeting market.

Meanwhile, one trend that took off in the decade that is sure to continue into the next is the focus on "green" building and operating practices throughout the industry. In 1998, the U.S. Green Building Council enacted its Leadership in Energy and Environmental Design (LEED) standards for rating buildings. The hotel industry was somewhat slow to adopt these eco-friendly building strategies, but when the University of Maryland Inn & Conference Center (a Marriott property) became the first LEED certified hotel in the United States in 2005, it opened the door for other hotels to follow.

Located next to Ground Zero, the Millenium Hilton shows just some of the horrible damage caused by the attacks of 9/11.

The first LEED Gold certification for a hotel was awarded to the Gaia Napa Valley Hotel & Spa in 2007, and in 2008 the first to receive LEED Platinum status was the Proximity Hotel in Greensboro, North Carolina. In the United States there are 17 hotels with LEED certification and more than 650 additional hospitality projects that are registered in the LEED certification process (as of Sept. 1, 2009.) Significantly, green hotel developments range from unique upscale projects such as the Montage Beverly Hills, California, to registered properties affiliated with mid-level brands such as Hampton Inn or Holiday Inn Express. In addition to the emphasis on environmentally friendly construction methods, hotel operators have also realized that changing certain operating practices can be positive for the bottom line. Many hotels throughout the country have adopted simple strategies such as replacing incandescent light bulbs with compact fluorescent light bulbs and allowing guests to request whether or not they want their bed linens and towels replaced daily, which reduces water and energy use and saves the hotel money. Early adopters of sustainable buildings and operations have also reaped significant public relations benefits through marketing their green strategies, but as the world engages in combating climate change, these practices will increasingly become mainstream for hotel developers and operators.

As the decade comes to a close, the lodging industry has experienced a roller-coaster ride, starting at the top of a cycle, dropping dramatically after the tech bubble burst and 9/11, then climbing again to an even higher peak before ending in a downward slide due to the economy. The challenges posed in coming years will keep hoteliers innovating and adapting, to find new ways to meet the demands of the world's travel enthusiasts. 100th

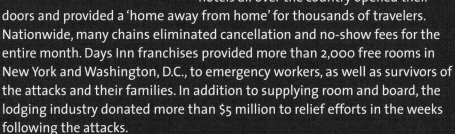

HOTELS & HISTORY

Shocking Events of the New Millennium

by Nicole Lichtenwalner

Between the tragedy of 9/11 and the natural disasters of 2004's tsunami and 2005's Hurricane Katrina, the new millennium has been plagued by an ongoing series of terrifying events. Hotels, however, have been one of the few constant sources of refuge. By providing the physical luxuries of room and board, hotels have helped heal the emotional wounds created by the shocking events of the new millennium.

As the Y2K buzz dwindled down, some were surprised that the world continued to function normally; the biggest shock, however, was yet to come. On a seemingly normal September morning, Americans' lives would be forever changed as they watched their televisions in horror as the World Trade Center towers crumbled.

Reflecting an industry true to its name, hotels all over the country opened their doors and provided a 'home away from home' for thousands of travelers. Nationwide, many chains eliminated cancellation and no-show fees for the entire month. Days Inn franchises provided more than 2,000 free rooms in New York and Washington, D.C., to emergency workers, as well as survivors of the attacks and their families. In addition to supplying room and board, the lodging industry donated more than $5 million to relief efforts in the weeks following the attacks.

As the world was slowly recovering from 9/11, another disaster was just around the corner. In 2005, Hurricane Katrina hurled itself at the United States. During and immediately after this tragedy, American hotels, in partnership with government agencies, accommodated more than 60,000 people. Although most states in the nation were housing Katrina victims, Houston took in the most evacuees — up to two-thirds of New Orleans' population. Once again, hotels rose to the occasion and served as impromptu homes, as places for victims to come together and share their experiences. ●

PHOTO BY NICHOLAS KAMM/AFP/GETTY IMAGES

2001

● **China Granted Normal Trade Status**

On December 27, The People's Republic of China was given normal trade status with the United States opening doors to investment in the country. Among the industries benefitting was the lodging industry as hotels found a new market to help spur growth.

● **Presidential Election Endures Recount**

Hotels in Florida, particularly in Dade County near Miami, filled up with media representatives as the nation's attention turned to the state and the recount of the votes in the highly contested 2000 presidential election. In the months following the election, the term "hanging chad" became part of the American lexicon. The election led to several changes and improvements in voting technology and policies.

2002

● **The Euro Makes its Debut**

On January 1, the European Union officially adopted a single currency for its 12 members at the time. By replacing legacy currency in those nations, commerce between European countries became more streamline. Likewise, it became easier for travelers to vacation in other nations throughout the continent and for overseas visitors to more easily move from place to place while touring Europe.

The Next 50

A Peek at Tomorrow

by Dr. Fred J. DeMicco

The future of the hospitality industry will feature a global marketplace with dynamic shifts in innovation. This timeline of travel probabilities includes challenges and opportunities facing tomorrow's travel industry.

According to experts, the 10 most important developments for the next decade include:

10. **In-air** Internet, cell phones, and text messaging
9. The continuing **decline of travel agents**
8. **Airport information kiosks**
7. **Universal Easy Pass:** Travelers' loyalty cards, credit/debit cards, and coupons will be stored on mobile phones.
6. **Technology eases security delays:** This includes retinal photos or other identifiers.
5. **RFID:** The behind-the-scenes uses of RFID (radio-frequency identification) will make a major difference in hospitality.
4. **Real-time translation:** Handheld speech translators will easily convert languages.
3. The **recovery** of the airline industry
2. **Aging of the Baby Boomer generation:** Their needs will dominate much of hospitality planning.
1. **China and India meet the world:** Experts predict an extra 75 million tourists every year from these emerging markets, with 50 million from the vast new Chinese middle class and 25 million from India.

Excerpts taken from *Hospitality and Travel 2015* by Marvin Cetron, Fred J. DeMicco & Owen Davies, published by the Educational Institute.

Looking Further

Other predictions are more speculative and visionary, since many of the following ideas projected by forecasters depend on technologies that have not yet been developed or perfected:

2015

- **INVISIBLE DIGITAL ASSISTANT:** Within a few years, well-equipped tourists will be carrying portable, cutting-edge speech translators that can convert multiple languages in real time.

- **WHO ARE YOU?** By 2012, passports and visas are expected to be replaced by biometric identity cards with records of fingerprints, retinal blood vessels, and other permanent, unique proof of identity.

- **A VIEW FROM ABOVE:** Experts predict that it will take less than a decade to build the first large-scale space tourism industry. Seats will sell for a lot less than the $20 million paid by recent travelers to visit the International Space Station.

- **GENERATIONS OF ENTREPRENEURS:** Throughout the world, people age 40 and under are starting businesses at a record rate. Expect a huge wave of new resorts, restaurants, tour operators and other travel services in the next two decades.

2020

- **FASTER THAN A SPEEDING BULLET TRAIN:** The world's fastest trains today operate at about 200 mph, although magnetic levitation trains have topped 300 mph. By 2020, the first 500-mph maglev trains will carry tourists around Japan, and from Los Angeles to Las Vegas.

- **VACATION REINVENTION:** Eventually, American workers will enjoy shorter work-weeks and mandatory vacations, as automation competition will continue to squeeze jobs from the economy. Cutting the work-week, and adding time off will result in a substantial burst of growth in tourism.

- **ECO-BACKLASH:** Hundreds of tourists trampling the Arctic tundra and other fragile environments will result in global protests and stringent limits on the number of tourists who can visit these destinations.

2030

- **BEANSTALK TO THE STARS:** A laser-propelled elevator will climb an enormous cable to a terminal where passengers can board spacecraft for the trip further out. Until recently, this was just a fantasy, but engineers say a space elevator could be completed within 15 years.

2040

- **UNDERSEA TRAVEL:** Presently, only one hotel is located under the sea, the two-bedroom Jules Underwater Resort in Key Largo, Florida. Four decades ahead, underwater hotels and restaurants will be almost common. Most will appear in shallow water, where sunlight penetrates to illuminate abundant life.

- **THE MAN IN/ON THE MOON:** The first permanent moon base is likely to appear in the 2030s. A decade later, it will be capable of accommodating up to 350 people, including 50 tourists. Thanks to a growing array of space elevators circling Earth's equator, a lunar jaunt will even be relatively affordable.

2050

- **UNIVERSAL ENGLISH:** Those aforementioned automatic translators will be useful for only 35 years or so. By 2050, more than 90 percent of the people in the world will speak English, at least as a second language. In tourist destinations, the number will be even higher.

2060

- **JOBS APLENTY:** Today, an estimated 14 percent of the world's people work in the hospitality industry. Tomorrow, it will be 25 percent. In part, this dramatic growth can be attributed to the explosion of leisure time when shorter work-weeks spread from Europe to the rest of the world. Fifty years from now, personal service could be the only job category that still requires human workers.

- **MEET AND GREET:** With a global Internet and social networking technology, who needs in-person meetings? Nearly everyone, as it turns out. Industry professionals should feel confident that there will be many more corporate and industrywide conventions in the future.

Editors

LEN VERMILLION
Editor

MARLA CIMINI
Managing Editor

PHIL HAYWARD
Contributing Editor

Len Vermillion is editor of *Lodging*, the official magazine of AH&LA. He has been an editor and writer for nearly 20 years, and also serves as editorial director of McNeill Group Inc. Prior to editing *Lodging*, he was an editor/writer for several business publications and has profiled some of the nation's top business leaders. He began his career as a reporter for daily newspapers. He lives with his wife, Nancy, in New Jersey.

Marla Cimini is a writer specializing in travel, food, and entertainment — and enjoys blending the three whenever possible. Her background includes managing public relations within Cendant's hotel division; as well as writing articles and speeches for AH&LA. A travel enthusiast, Marla's frequent globetrotting adventures always lead her back home to Cherry Hill, New Jersey, where she lives with her husband, Chris.

Phil Hayward is chief communications officer of the National Recreation & Park Association in Ashburn, Virginia. Until recently, he was editor of *Lodging*. Previously, he was managing editor of *Air & Space/Smithsonian* magazine and managing editor of *Mid-Atlantic Country* magazine. He graduated from Eisenhower College with a degree in history and lives in Alexandria, Virginia, with his wife and daughter.

ROBERT V. ALLEGRINI

Robert V. Allegrini is a hospitality executive, author, and civic leader who is currently vice president of communications of the Americas at Hilton Hotel Corporation. In this capacity, he manages the regional public relations team serving all the Hilton brands' properties throughout the western hemisphere.

FRED J. DIMICCO

Dr. Fred J.DiMicco, Ph.D., is professor and ARAMARK Chair in the Department of Hotel, Restaurant, and Institutional Management at the University of Delaware. He is author and co-author of more than 100 publications in the area of hospitality and tourism management.

MATT BRINN

Matt Brinn is a writer who graduated from The College of New Jersey in Trenton. With a bachelor's of arts in history and a penchant for traveling abroad, he is aiming toward a career in political journalism. He currently lives in Hammonton, New Jersey.

GENE FIDUCIA

Gene Fiducia is a teacher of preschool disabled children, as well as an architecture and design enthusiast. He and his wife have traveled the world extensively. His first travel essay chronicles his two thousand-mile, four-month trek along the Appalachian Trail in 1973. Today, he prefers hotels when he vacations.

HARVEY CHIPKEN

Harvey Chipkin has been writing about the travel industry for more than 35 years — specializing in hotels. He has written for *Lodging*, as well as numerous travel industry publications. He has been a contributor to *Travel & Leisure*, *Gourmet*, and several newspapers. He lives in New Jersey with his wife, Janet.

JOY GUERMONT

Joy Guermont has a degree in English literature and is certified in English and elementary education. Traveling over the years, she has had the opportunity to experience various destinations and accommodations ranging from B&Bs to luxury hotels. She is a dedicated mother working in the educational field and enjoys writing in her spare time.

ALEX CORINI

Alex Corini has been informing, entertaining, and provoking those reading, viewing, or listening to his musings for years. While a communications major at Rider University, he was involved with creative projects in radio, TV, and film. He is currently a sound engineer working in the music industry.

JOORI JEON

Joori Jeon is executive vice president and chief financial officer for AH&LA, and president and COO of its not-for-profit affiliate, AH&LEF. Her responsibilities include establishing financial policies and practices; directing finance, human resources, and office administration; and developing and implementing a budget to support the association's strategic plan.

Contributors

LEDA KOPACH

Leda Kopach is a writer and editor currently serving as communications manager for Drexel University's LeBow College of Business. She has written extensively on the travel, lodging, and beauty and spa industries. She lives in Bucks County, Pennsylvania, with her husband and daughter.

A. COREY LIMBACH

A. Corey Limbach has 25 years of experience as a market and financial consultant in the hospitality industry. Based in the San Francisco Bay area, he has been involved with projects all over the country as well as internationally. He is currently working toward his certificate in Green Building.

BERENICE MENDEZ

Berenice Mendez is a freelance writer living in the Chicagoland area. She studied human resources in her college years, but has a background in hospitality. She also enjoys reading and writing poetry.

JAY KRUPP

Jay Krupp is the director of educational and custom services at Newmarket International, where he is involved in technology education, specializing in hospitality software. He has experience in hotel operations with luxury hotels, including the Four Seasons Chicago.

ROBERT MANDELBAUM

Robert Mandelbaum is the director of research information services for PKF Hospitality Research. He is responsible for producing the firm's annual *Trends in the Hotel Industry* report. He is a member of AH&LA's Financial Management Committee and holds a bachelor's degree in science from Cornell University.

MELISSA MIJARES

Melissa Mijares holds a bachelor's degree in English from the College of New Jersey in Trenton, New Jersey. An avid traveler, she continues to explore the world and works as a professional writer.

NICOLE LICHTENWALNER

Nicole Lichtenwalner is studying at Saint Joseph's University in Philadelphia. She is a business major with a love for writing. Her hobbies include modeling, traveling, and spending time with her friends and family.

DAWN MARCHADIER

Dawn Marchadier is a biomedical research project manager from Montreal, Canada, who now lives in New Jersey, but would rather be exploring the globe from a home base in the south of France. She has traveled extensively along the highways and back roads of North America and Europe.

ANDREA MORABITO

Andrea Morabito is a freelance writer living in New York City. She is a journalism graduate of the Newhouse School at Syracuse University, and her work has been published in several magazines and online outlets, including *Hour Detroit* magazine, TheBusinessInsider.com, and RecessionWire.com.

SANDRA PERILLI

Sandra Perilli is a writer and former educator living in New Jersey. She enjoys writing screenplays and is a member of the Society of Children's Book Writers and Illustrators. She is the founder of FolioFLY, a company that helps teachers transition their students between school and work.

CHERYL COURTNEY SEMICK

Cheryl Courtney Semick is a freelance writer, editor, and president of Semick Inc., in Peoria, Illinois. She is co-author of one book and soon-to-be author of three. She is impassioned by the power of story to positively affect change in the human heart, mind, and soul.

GEORGE E. VONALLMEN

George E. VonAllmen is the president of HeadStand Consulting and a 30-year veteran of the hospitality industry. He provides businesses with innovative sales and marketing assistance, ranging from retail and hospitality to alternative energy.

TREANNA SANTILLO

Treanna Santillo is a graduate of Saint Joseph's University in Philadelphia with a bachelor's degree in business administration. She enjoys reading and writing in her free time, and is currently working for a real estate property management company in New Haven, Connecticut.

ROBERT L. STEELE, III

Robert L. Steele, III, is president and COO of the American Hotel & Lodging Educational Institute (EI). He oversees the day-to-day operations of EI, and develops the overall vision and strategies in conjunction with the board of trustees. A longtime hotelier, he was chairman of AH&LA in 2007.

LYDIA WESTBROOK

Lydia Westbrook has served as director of the AH&LA Information Center since its move to University of Houston in 2002. She holds a master's of hospitality management degree and teaches tourism at the Conrad N. Hilton College at UH. She has earned the Certified Hospitality Educator (CHE) designation from the AH&LA Educational Institute.

SHELLEY SEALE

Shelley Seale is a freelance writer based in Austin, Texas, but she vagabonds throughout the world whenever possible. She is a contributor to several major publications. Her new book, *The Weight of Silence*, follows her journeys into the orphanages and slums of India where millions of children live without families. Her mantra is "travel with a purpose."

CHERYL-ANNE STURKEN

Cheryl-Anne Sturken was born in British Guyana and grew up in Barbados. She was senior editor with *Meetings & Conventions* magazine for 15 years. In 2001, she won the American Society of Business Publications' Editorial Excellence award. She lives in Katonah, New York, with her husband, two daughters, and several pets.

R. MARK WOODWORTH

R. Mark Woodworth is executive vice president of PKF Consulting and president of PKF Hospitality Research. He is responsible for activities in the Southeast and Caribbean, as well as developing benchmarking and forecast reports. He holds both a bachelor's degree and a master's degree from Cornell University.

INDEX

INDEX

Organizations

People

ACKNOWLEDGEMENTS

The American Hotel & Lodging Association (AH&LA) wishes to acknowledge with gratitude the many people and organizations who contributed to the success of this project. AH&LA also wishes to acknowledge the contributions of the numerous individuals who have volunteered their time and resources to ensuring a successful centennial celebration.

AH&LA Centennial Committee

- John J. Russell, Jr. (Chair)
- Brad Aldrich, MHS
- Walt Baker
- Vinita Bhatia
- Lisa Campagne
- John R. Campbell
- Ronald F. Cichy
- Roger W. Conner
- Thomas J Corcoran, Jr.
- Michael Davidson
- Dorothy Dowling
- James Gaffigan
- David Goldstone, MHS
- Pam Inman, IOM, CAE
- Caryn Kboudi
- David Kong
- Liz Kuvinka
- John T. Lee
- Joe Martin, CHA
- Joseph A. McInerney, CHA
- John K. Merkin
- Kimberly Miles, CMP
- David Peikin
- Thomas J. Polski
- Kathryn C. Potter
- Trisha A. Pugal, CAE
- Matthew R. Schwarz, MHS
- Jessica Soklow
- Robert L. Steele, III
- Netanya A. Stutz
- Lucy Subhasiriwatana
- David Trumble

Photo Credits

- Accor Hotels
- American Hotel & Lodging Association
- American Hotel & Lodging Educational Foundation
- American Hotel & Lodging Educational Institute
- American Hotel & Lodging Information Center/ University of Houston
- American Express
- Andaz West Hollywood
- Best Western International Inc.
- Carlson Hotels Worldwide
- Choice Hotels International
- Fairmont Hotels & Resorts
- Gaia Napa Valley Hotel and Spa
- Hilton Hotels Corporation
- Hyatt Hotels Corporation
- Intercontinental Hotels Group
- Joseph and Joan Cimini
- Kimpton Hotels & Restaurants
- Las Vegas News Bureau
- Loews Hotels & Resorts
- Mandarin-Oriental Hotel Group
- Marriott International Inc.
- Nicholas Kamm/AFP/Getty Images
- The Beverly Hills Hotel
- The Hay-Adams
- The Governor Hotel
- The Waldorf=Astoria
- Smith Travel Research
- Starwood Hotels & Resorts
- Wyndham Hotel Group